SOFT FURNISHINGS FOR DOLLHOUSES

Awaken your fantasies
and build on your daydreams. . .

Lael and Terry dedicate this book—especially the sewing room—to the memory of their mother,
Florence Stephens Combe, a couturère who was truly ahead of her time.

LAEL COMBE FURGESON
TERRY COMBE JOHNSON

SOFT FURNISHINGS FOR DOLLHOUSES

215 Enchanting NoSew Designs & Patterns

Sterling Publishing Co., Inc. New York
A Sterling/Chapelle Book

Book builders: *Chapelle Ltd.*

OWNER: Jo Packham

DESIGN/LAYOUT EDITOR:
Leslie Ridenour

PHOTOGRAPHER:
Kevin Dilley for Hazen Photography

PHOTOGRAPHIC STYLIST: Peggy Bowers

FINISH CARPENTER:
Al Borman of Auburn, CA

STAFF:
Marie Barber, Ann Bear,
Areta Bingham, Kass Burchett,
Rebecca Christensen, Holly Fuller,
Marilyn Goff, Shirley Heslop,
Holly Hollingsworth, Sherry Hoppe,
Shawn Hsu, Susan Jorgensen,
Pauline Locke, Barbara Milburn,
Linda Orton, Karmen Quinney,
Cindy Stoeckl

Due to the limited amount of space available, we must print our patterns at a reduced size in order to give our patrons the maximum number of projects possible in our publications. We believe the quality and quantity of our patterns will compensate for any inconvenience this may cause.

Library of Congress Cataloging-in-Publication Data

Furgeson, Lael Combe.
    Soft furnishings for dollhouses : 215 enchanting nosew designs & patterns/Lael Combe Furgeson, Terry Combe Johnson.
        p.   cm.
    Includes index
    ISBN 0-8069-4286 X
    1. Doll furniture.   2. Dollhouses.   3. Textile crafts.
    4. Decoration and ornament.   I. Johnson, Terry Combe.   II. Title
    TT175.5.F87   1999
    745.592'3–dc21
                                                            98-40462
                                                                CIP

1   3   5   7   9   10   8   6   4   2

A Sterling/Chapelle Book

First paperback edition published in 2000 by
Sterling Publishing Company, Inc.
387 Park Avenue South, New York, N.Y. 10016
© 1999 by Chapelle Ltd.
Distributed in Canada by Sterling Publishing
c/o Canadian Manda Group, One Atlantic Avenue, Suite 105
Toronto, Ontario, Canada M6K 3E7
Distributed in Great Britain and Europe by Cassell PLC
Wellington House, 125 Strand, London WC2R 0BB, England
Distributed in Australia by Capricorn Link (Australia) Pty Ltd.
P.O. Box 6651, Baulkham Hills, Business Centre, NSW 2153, Australia
Printed in China
All rights reserved

Sterling ISBN 0-8069-4286-X Trade
                    0-8069-4973-2 Paper

Every effort has been made to ensure that all of the information in this book is accurate. However, due to differing conditions, tools, and individual skills, the publisher cannot be responsible for any injuries, losses, and/or any other damages which may result from the use of the information in this book.

If you have any questions or comments or would like information about any specialty products featured in this book, please contact:

Chapelle Ltd., Inc.
P.O. Box 9252
Ogden, UT 84409

Phone: (801)621-2777 Fax: (801)621-2788
e-mail: Chapelle1@aol.com

Behind the seams: *about the authors*

For sisters, Lael Combe Furgeson and Terry Combe Johnson, this book captures the elusive threads of past and present.

Fabric, textures, and creative energy have always been a part of the authors' lives, for these rich elements filled the sewing room where, as children (pictured at right in black and white), they played and watched their mother create exquisite one-of-a-kind wedding gowns from rich silks, slipper satins, and laces trimmed with seed pearls and iridescent sequins.

Lael, encouraged at an early age by an aunt who was an art teacher, drew, colored, and painted throughout her youth. In high school and college, she signed up for anything that had to do with art. The result is Lael's rich and diverse art background.

She operated an interior design studio in San Jose, California for seven years before moving to Boston, Massachusetts in 1983. There she designed "high-end" painted art for a well-known manufacturer of fabric paint. Her work was featured in television ads, at trade shows, and on paint labels. She also authored six how-to books about creating "wearable art " before returning to California where she currently resides.

Terry's passion lies in the three-dimensional world of bronze sculpture. She loves to physically shape and manipulate her work and finds tremendous satisfaction in being able to walk around the object and see it from all different angles. Just as a writer's words communicate themes and emotions, Terry's sculptures speak for her. One of her commissioned bronze sculptures, "Let's Try Again," is a charming life-sized rendition of a girl helping a younger child, who has fallen, to his feet to skate again. It is located at The Ice Sheet ice skating arena in Ogden, Utah, a site that will host skating events during the 2002 Winter Olympics.

Terry enjoys teaching both sculpting and watercolor classes. For her, the best part of these classes comes when "there are no more questions—verbalization stops, visualization begins, and creativity takes over."

After years of working independently, Lael and Terry have combined their respective talents to re-create one of the joys of their youth. They compare constructing the soft furnishings in this dollhouse to sewing a fine satin seam. The many "stitches" in this partnership are reflected in each and every tiny piece.

Open house: *contents*

General Information   8

Provence Kitchen   16

Living & Dining Room   28

Garden Bathroom   44

Master Suite   56

Sewing Room   76

Pretty-n-pink Nursery   88

Whimsy Bedroom   102

Patio Furniture   118

Acknowledgments   127
Metric Conversion Chart   127
Index   128

General Information

hints

scissors

miniature

glue

fabric

scale

pins

materials

paint

iron

compass

tools

Introduction

Our dollhouse and each collection of miniature "soft furnishings" in it are the result of our own enchanting childhood daydreams. Our wish is to awaken your fantasies and help you build upon your own daydreams.

Most of the instructions for individual soft furnishings projects in this book avoid calling for specific fabrics and measurements. Instead, we have given you more generalized directions for making the tiny furnishings so that you can adapt them to your own design style and dollhouse dimensions.

We have placed many items within our dollhouse that are so simple, we did not provide instructions for them. We have also given you an artist's rendering of "redecorating" ideas for each room in the house. By combining these examples with your imagination and a little ribbon, paint, sculpting clay, or dried flowers, you can create 150 additional projects.

glue
fabric
scale
pins
iron

General Information

When we first removed this dollhouse from its box, we were so excited with the design and flavor of the "shell" of the house. We immediately began deciding which rooms would be which for the imaginary family living in the house.

Our excitement began with the front opening, which meant that it would not have to be turned around to the back when someone

Right: *It was easy to create an item of interest by tying up these tiny hatboxes with a bright red wired ribbon.*

Below left: *The delicate lace edging on the crib canopy was made from a hand-cut handkerchief.*

wanted to "play" with it. Only the front porch panels had to be folded back to be able to step into our magical play world.

We started with the living room and dining room on the main floor, planning for any entertaining our little family might do—making it cozy, yet flexible enough for Christmas-time gatherings and a big old-fashioned tree.

The kitchen had to be one of creativity. Since we both like to cook and entertain, it had to be clean and crisp—looking very well organized — in order to inspire the imaginary Mother to cook and to have her children join in when she is baking cookies and other treats.

We placed the master suite above the living room. We knew we just had to find a beautiful bed with a canopy overhead—the bed we had both dreamed of having one day, a quiet retreat for reading a love story. The cheerful buttery yellow color was a natural choice for the couple to wake up to as well as a beautiful background for the bed made of dark mahogany wood. Staying true to our design style, we trimmed the lamp shade with tiny tassels and hung pictures on the walls with moiré ribbon bows.

We wanted the bathroom next to the master suite to feel "garden-like." We were trying to accomplish a fresh, open feeling where we could imagine small children enjoying a bubble bath in the large tub. After the bath, they could dry themselves with thick fluffy towels. We used ribbon and adhesive to create a lattice effect on the walls.

On the other side of the master suite came the sewing room retreat. We feel that every woman should have a place or an outlet wherein she can express her secret desires, whether it be sewing, knitting, or anything else she can create with her hands. We created this room with our mother in mind. So many memories came rushing back to us as we tried to replicate the place where we spent so much time as children.

We thought it would be fitting to add a "Red Pot" to accent the sewing room. As young girls, we watched our mother place her heavy red pot on the satins and silks to keep them from sliding off her special cutting table.

Above the sewing room is the whimsy bedroom which we created for our little family's teenage girl. The room is full of wonderful colors that reflect a sense of adventure and zest for experiencing life. You can believe that the girl who lives in this room is full of life and fun and is happy with her existence.

No dollhouse would be complete without a baby's nursery. The canopy crib, toys, and rocking chair make it easy for the new mother to comfort the small child who has awakened during the night.

We haven't decided which room was most fun to "soft furnish," but the Patio gave us a special feeling— even down to the placement of the magazines in the back pockets of the chairs and lounge.

We totally enjoyed our time with this house from the day it arrived in our hands until the day we had to let it go to be photographed for this book. We had a wonderful time together reliving old memories and creating new ones. You might say that we "lived" in this house and we felt "homeless" when it left us.

Fabric Tips

Look for fabrics that are not stiff but have a nice fall or drape to them when held in the hand. They will fall nicer on windows, spreads, and furniture when they are soft. If a piece of fabric, such as cotton, which can sometimes be on the stiff side, is desired, try softening it in a sink full of water with fabric softener added. Rinse, dry, and press flat before using.

Woolens fray easily and are the best textiles to use when a fringed edge is desired.

Some fabrics, such as ultrasuede, can be purchased by the pound in very small pieces.

If there is a custom fabric mill in your area, you can often find sales representatives who will donate very small fabric samples.

Above: *Various general materials needed for completing soft furnishings projects.*

General Materials Needed

The materials in the following list and in the photograph on the opposite page are used generally throughout the book. Make certain to refer to individual materials list or "Things You Will Need" for completing each project.

All purpose adhesive
Batting: flat (used for quilting); fluffy (used for stuffing)
Dowels: ⅛"-dia.; ³⁄₁₆"-dia.
Fabric marking pen
Fabric stiffening medium
Fine-grit sandpaper and 2" x 3" block of wood (for sanding block)
Fusible liquid adhesive with long tip applicator
Hot-glue gun (with low and high temperature to accommodate small and tight areas) and glue sticks
Iron and ironing board
Mattboard (as used in picture framing)
Measuring tape
Metal ruler
Miter box and saw for miniatures (for sawing moldings, etc.)
Paintbrushes: ¼" flat, soft bristles; ½" flat, soft bristles; round, small soft point; 1" sponge
Pencil
Permanent liquid adhesive with long tip applicator
Pins
Pressing cloth: 8" square (made of synthetic plastic-type material to protect iron from fusible liquid adhesive)
Scissors: craft; fabric
Sewing needles and coordinating thread
Spray adhesive
Straight-edge razor blade
Tweezers (with smallest available point)
Water jar (for rinsing brushes)
Wood glue

Above: *Useful items that may be kept on hand.*

Things That are Useful

Beads
Buttons: small; tiny
Charms
Jewelry pieces
Lace and trims: small, narrow
Ribbons: small amounts in many colors
Silk flower and leaf pieces

Possible Places to Find Tiny Items

Craft stores are an invaluable source for finding charms, beads, jewelry findings, silk flowers, paints, paintbrushes, wood dowels, ornaments, and sculpting clays.

Dollhouse specialty stores carry furniture in a variety of woods and fabrics. Decorator rugs and carpeting are also available.

Thrift stores may offer second-hand doll-house furniture, doilies, and vintage fabrics for use in soft furnishings.

Vintage stores often have vintage fabrics, baby clothes, handkerchiefs, napkins, old laces, trims, and ribbons for sale.

Fabric stores are the first places we look for remnants of fabrics, laces, ribbons, braids, samples of fabric, buttons, and scraps by the pound.

Remember to look in your mother's, aunt's, or grandmother's sewing drawers or baskets for vintage fabrics and notions.

Note: Save any little scraps on hand, because so little is needed for soft dollhouse decorating.

Above: *Use liquid adhesives to adhere surfaces and seal seams.*

Helpful Hints

A sewing machine is not necessary for making the soft furnishings projects in this book, as nearly all projects are completed using a hand-sewing needle and thread, or liquid adhesives, such as Liqui-Fuse™ or Fabri-Tac™ (used almost exclusively for these projects). The first is a fusible liquid adhesive, used with an iron. The latter is a permanent liquid adhesive, used for gluing. Make certain to follow manufacturer's instructions for use of both types of liquid adhesive.

When adhering two surfaces together or sealing a seam with fusible liquid adhesives, cover ironing board with a piece of fabric about 24" square in the area you will be working to protect ironing board cover from adhesives.

Also, always use a plastic-type pressing cloth between iron and project fabric to avoid scorching fabrics and to keep the iron free of adhesives. To seal properly, heat must be applied to the project for at least 30-45 seconds.

Liqui-Fuse™ can be sealed with an iron when in wet or dry state with equal effectiveness, which is helpful when the project can't be ironed immediately.

Above: *Most items needed to create these tiny projects can be found in the sewing room.*

Making a Circle Using a Compass

1. Fold a piece of fabric in half and then in half again, pinning to hold in place. Divide required diameter measurement in half. Using a measuring tape, measure this dimension down from folded point of fabric along the fold and, using a fabric marking pen, mark for placement. Attach one end of a piece of string to the tip of the marking pen. Hold opposite end of string in place on folded point and move marking pen from mark on fold to raw edge of fabric, holding string taut and drawing a curve.

2. Using fabric scissors, cut fabric along drawn line. Unfold for a circle.

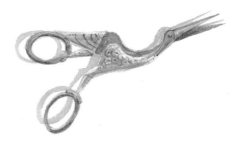

Provence Kitchen

dishes

napkins

breakfast

dinner

cooking

pots

cupboards

spices

canisters

utensils

baking

homemade

More than any other room, the kitchen is the center of the home—all other family activities start here. It is the place where Mother is fixing supper when children arrive home from school. She lets them help her peel carrots and potatoes while they tell her all about what's new at school. The family gathers around the table for meals and to talk about the day's happenings.

Copper pots and pans and all sorts of kitchen gadgets are kept near the stove. Treasured books, that hold Grandma's "secret" recipes, are at arm's reach.

The scents of long ago Sunday mornings—sizzling bacon, hot cinnamon rolls, and fresh-printed "funny papers"— drift off into the upper rooms of the house.

Fresh-squeezed orange juice, invites hungry little ones to the table. The scent of mini muffins, baking in the oven, wraps the family in the warmth of home.

Provence Kitchen

The combination of delicate floral prints, bold checks, and cheery polk-a-dots produce a room with a French flair that is fresh, clean, and inviting.

A checked ribbon lines the corner cupboard, drawing the visitors' attention to three tiny teapots shaped like cakes and pies that fit perfectly on lace-covered shelves.

The "china" is proudly displayed in the hutch for all to see. These custom-made little cups and dishes match the provincial linens.

Simple runners for the table and refrigerator top coordinate with chair cushions. These dress up the otherwise plain furniture, helping to create a dining ensemble with a feel for the country.

Above: *Adhere tiny sprigs of various herbs to a short length of twine to dress up a bare wall.*

Left: *The kitchen is in order—prepared for any company that may come to visit.*

Opposite: *The doors of the cupboard are open wide to show off a prized collection of tiny teapots.*

Lace trimmings: *pâtisserie cupboard*

YOU WILL NEED:
- Measuring tape
- Miniature cupboard
- Panel lace with scalloped edge
- Paper for pattern
- Permanent liquid adhesive
- Ribbon: 1"-wide
- Scissors: craft; fabric

MAKING THE PROJECT:

1. Using measuring tape, measure from one front side of cupboard, to back corner, and to opposite front side of cupboard. Using fabric scissors, cut ribbon to those dimensions. Trim ribbon to fit height between shelves.

2. Fit ribbon between shelves and secure to sides of cupboard with a thin line of permanent liquid adhesive. Repeat for each shelf.

3. Make paper pattern for shelf by placing paper on shelf and using your finger nail to score along sides and front of shelf. Add ½" to the front side of the triangle for scallop to drop beyond shelf edge. Using craft scissors, cut pattern along score marks.

4. Place front side of shelf pattern along scalloped edge of lace. Using fabric scissors, cut out. Fit lace to shelf and secure with a thin line of permanent liquid adhesive. Repeat for each shelf.

Note: When covering bottom shelf, cut off overhanging scallop so cupboard doors can close.

Tea rose: *kitchen china*

YOU WILL NEED:
- Acrylic paint: to match decor
- Découpage medium
- Fabric: cotton with tiny floral print (2–3")
- Paintbrushes: ½" flat; small round
- Scissors: fabric
- Sculpting clay: color desired for base color of dishes (1 pkg.)

MAKING THE PROJECT:

1. Roll a bit of clay into six marble-sized balls for plates.

2. Press each ball firmly to flatten to a round shape. Hold up to cupboard to check for height fit.

3. Roll a bit of clay into six pea-sized balls for cups. Poke one side of each ball with end of paintbrush handle to create the well of the cup. Slightly flatten the bottom of each cup so it will sit. Pinch one side for handle.

4. Bake clay plates and cups, following manufacturer's instructions. Allow to cool.

5. Using small round paintbrush, paint dots and swirls on plates and cups.

6. Using fabric scissors, cut out fabric flowers.

7. Using flat paintbrush, apply découpage medium onto a plate. Center and place one fabric flower onto plate. Apply découpage medium over entire plate to secure fabric to clay surface. Repeat for all plates.

Note: Experiment sculpting with more complex shapes, making other china service pieces, such as a soup tureen or platter.

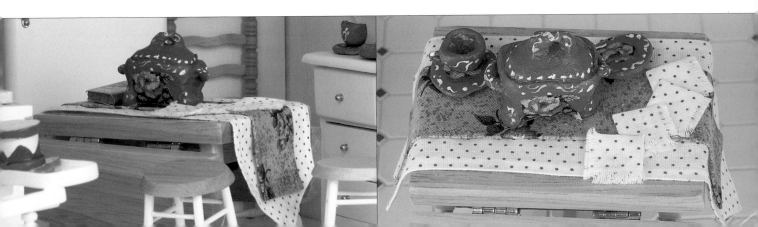

Daily accent: *table runner*

- Fabric: cotton prints, 6" square (2)
- Fabric scissors
- Fusible liquid adhesive
- Iron and ironing board
- Measuring tape
- Miniature table
- Pressing cloth

Making the project:

1. Using measuring tape, measure tabletop length and width dimensions. Using fabric scissors, cut one print fabric 4" longer than tabletop and ½" less than its width. Cut each corner off fabric, making a point in the center at each short end. Place fabric, wrong side up, on work surface. Apply a thin line of fusible liquid adhesive ⅛" from each edge. Fold each edge over ¼" and, using iron and pressing cloth, press to seal edges.

2. Using fabric scissors, cut second print fabric ½" narrower in width than the first print fabric. Place fabric, wrong side up, on work surface. Apply a thin line of fusible liquid adhesive ⅛" from each edge. Fold each edge over ¼" and, using iron and pressing cloth, press to seal edges.

3. Center and place smaller runner on top of larger runner. Place runners on table.

Crumb catchers: *napkins*

You will need:
- Fabric: cotton print (6" square)
- Fabric scissors
- Iron and ironing board
- Pressing cloth

Making the project:

1. Using fabric scissors, cut each napkin piece to 1¼" square. Pull threads all around napkin to fringe edges about ⅛". Fold each napkin in half, then in half again, and, using iron and pressing cloth, press for permanent folds. Place on table, overlapping as desired.

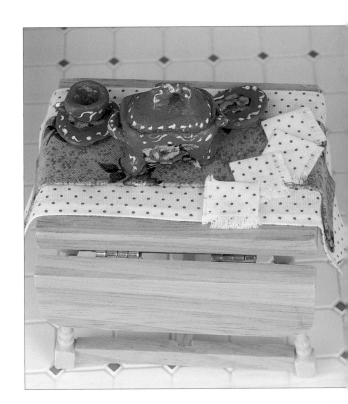

Petite cheques: *chair cushion*

SEE PHOTO ON PAGE 22.

YOU WILL NEED:
- Batting: flat
- Fabric: cotton prints (2)
- Fabric scissors
- Fusible liquid adhesive
- Iron and ironing board
- Measuring tape
- Miniature chair
- Pressing cloth

MAKING THE PROJECT:

1. Using measuring tape, measure chair from front to back, and double the measurement. Measure chair width, adding ¼". Using fabric scissors, cut fabric to those dimensions.

2. Fold, with right sides together, so short ends meet. Apply a thin line of fusible liquid adhesive along right side of side edges and, using iron and pressing cloth, press to seal edges. Turn right side out, creating a pouch. Using fabric scissors, cut batting to fit inside fabric pouch. Stuff with batting. Turn remaining raw edges to inside, apply a thin line of fusible liquid adhesive, and, using iron and pressing cloth, press to seal edges.

3. If desired, using fabric scissors, cut a motif from coordinating fabric. Apply a thin line of fusible liquid adhesive around outside edge of wrong side of motif. Center motif, right side up, on top of chair cushion and, using iron and pressing cloth, press to seal edges.

Cheques & fleurs: *refrigerator runner*

YOU WILL NEED:
- Fabric: cotton print (1½" x 7")
- Miniature refrigerator

MAKING THE PROJECT:

1. Pull threads all around refrigerator runner to fringe edges about ⅛". Lay runner over top of refrigerator.

Simply sheer: *window treatment*

YOU WILL NEED:
- Acrylic paint: to match window
- Dowel: ⅛"-dia., 1" longer than width of window
- Eyescrews: gold, (2)
- Fabric: soft cotton batiste (3" x 13")
- Fusible liquid adhesive
- Hammer
- Hot-glue gun and glue sticks
- Iron and ironing board
- Nail: tiny
- Paintbrush: ¼" flat
- Pencil
- Pressing cloth
- Sculpting clay: coordinating color for dowel ball ends

MAKING THE PROJECT:

1. Place fabric, wrong side up, on work surface. Apply a thin line of fusible liquid adhesive ⅛" from short edges of fabric. Fold edges over ¼" and, using iron and pressing cloth, press to seal edges.

2. Apply a thin line of fusible liquid adhesive ⅛" from one long edge of fabric. Fold edge over ¼" and press to seal edge. When cool, apply a thin line of fusible liquid adhesive ⅛" from sealed edge of fabric. Fold edge over again ½" and press to create bottom hem.

3. Apply a thin line of fusible liquid adhesive ⅛" from remaining long edge of fabric. Fold edge over ¼" and press to seal, leaving a channel for dowel to thread through.

4. Using paintbrush, paint dowel. Allow to dry. Thread painted dowel through channel.

5. Hold dowel up to window and, using pencil, mark placement for eyescrews on wall. Allow at least ¼" from each end of dowel to accommodate ball ends.

6. Using hammer and tiny nail, make a small hole at each mark. Screw eyescrews into holes. Insert dowel, one end at a time, into eyescrews.

7. Roll a bit of clay into two pea-sized balls. Poke each ball midway with one end of dowel. Remove dowel. Bake clay balls, following manufacturer's instructions. Allow to cool.

8. Using hot-glue gun, adhere one clay ball to each end of dowel.

Le coq: *redecorating ideas*

Give the French country kitchen a farm-house-style makeover. This artist's rendition shows how to achieve the look by adding simple decorative elements specific to the style, such as placing shelves around the perimeter of the room for holding knickknacks.

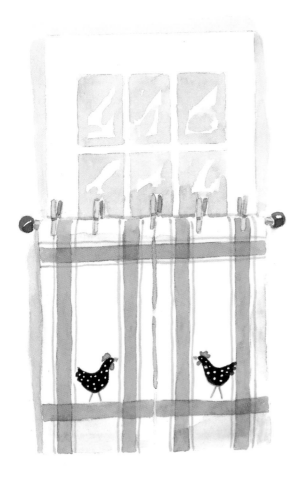

Above: *Use purchased miniature towels for curtains. Stencil chickens onto towels to match wall decor. Peg towels onto dowel with miniature clothespins.*

Right: *Stencil chickens onto walls. Make breads and cakes from sculpting clay.*

Living &
Dining Room

In the living room, wassail is waiting in the silver punch bowl to take away the chill of winter.

Family photos and favorite works of art caress the fabric-covered walls. A prized oriental-style porcelain vase sits, accented by Williamsburg plates, in a hutch that also holds a warm blanket.

The very formal white-on-white damask and rich cherry wood furnishings create the ideal setting for pleasant conversation and entertaining guests. The comfortable sofa and chair can be replaced with little folding chairs to accommodate friends and family who come to hear a violin recital for one of the children.

Each one has a place at the dining room table where a gourmet meal, including buttery carrots, double stuffed baked potatoes, and herb roasted chicken, will be served. And to top it all off—chocolate turnovers for dessert.

entertain

visitors

tea service

books

clock

throws

silverware

paintings

area rug

candelabra

formal

throws

area rug

paintings

candelabra

clock

Living &
Dining Room

Deep, rich colors and clean lines yield a dramatic effect in this large room. Thoughtful placement of area rugs on the hardwood floors and wainscotting on the walls creates a timeless look.

A luxurious mohair blanket and matching crocheted doilies draped over the sofa and table soften the room's decor, making it a comfortable living area.

Gilded picture frames, a gold candelabra, and a silver tea service—accessories to the fine wood furniture—catch the light and the visitor's interest, while a stately grandfather clock sits in the middle of the room for all to see and hear, chiming the hours away.

Above: *The dainty tea service adds to the intimate atmosphere created by the classic furniture placed in this sitting area.*

Below: *The openness of the dining and living area allows for both casual and formal entertaining of family and friends.*

Mild manners: *puddled table covering*

YOU WILL NEED:
- Bowl: large, 2 qt.
- Cardboard: thin, 4" square (2)
- Doily: 5"-dia.
- Fabric: cotton print (18" square)
- Fabric stiffening medium
- Hot-glue gun and glue sticks
- Measuring tape
- Miniature square table
- Permanent liquid adhesive
- Scissors: craft; fabric
- Waxed paper

MAKING THE PROJECT:

1. Using measuring tape, measure tabletop width and add ½" for diameter of circular tabletop. Using craft scissors, cut two circles from cardboard to those dimensions.

2. Using hot-glue gun, apply glue liberally to one side of one circle. Adhere to remaining circle. Apply glue to tabletop. Center and adhere circle to tabletop.

3. Place table upright on work surface. Refer to Making a Circle Using a Compass on page 15. Using measuring tape, measure from floor on one side, up to tabletop, across circle, and down opposite side to floor for diameter of circular tablecloth, adding 2½" for draping. Using fabric scissors, cut fabric to those dimensions.

4. Place fabric circle over table to check for fit. The fabric should puddle on the floor at base of table.

5. Pour fabric stiffening medium into bowl.

Place fabric circle in medium, stirring to thoroughly coat.

6. Gently remove fabric from bowl, drawing it through your fingers to squeeze out excess medium.

7. Place fabric, wrong side up, on work surface covered with waxed paper. Fold fabric over ¼" around edge and finger-press to secure "hem" in place.

8. Turn table upside down. Center and place table on fabric circle. Turn fabric and table right side up as one and place on work surface, allowing fabric to fall to waxed paper. Using your fingers, arrange folds of

fabric and hemline, allowing to puddle all around table. Allow outside to dry. Turn table and fabric upside down as one and allow inside to dry.

9. Center and place doily on tabletop and adhere with permanent liquid adhesive.

White on white: *custom sofa & chairs*

YOU WILL NEED:
- Batting: fluffy
- Braided fringe: cotton, fluffy (¾ yd.)
- Cardboard: thin (5" x 10")
- Fabric: soft, drapable, (⅓ yd.)
- Hot-glue gun and glue sticks
- Measuring tape
- Miniature sofa and chair forms
- Paper: white (1 sheet)
- Pencil
- Permanent liquid adhesive
- Pins
- Scissors: craft; fabric

MAKING THE PROJECT:
1. Using fabric scissors, cut an 11" square from fabric. Fold in half, then in half again. Mark center point with a pin.

2. Using measuring tape, measure sofa form to find center point at back top. Refer to Centered Fabric Diagram. Line up center point of fabric with center point on sofa, placing fabric square diagonally on sofa.

Centered
Fabric
Diagram

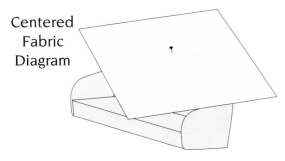

3. Using hot-glue gun, apply a ½" line of glue in crease where the front of sofa back and cushion meet. Using your fingers, smooth fabric down the sofa back and onto glue.

4. Temporarily fold fabric from back toward front. Dot-glue down ½" from top of sofa along back side. Refer to Back of Sofa Diagram. Using fingers, smooth fabric up and over sofa back onto glue. Slightly gather fabric to cover top of back, working from one side to the other and toward corners and arms. Using hot-glue gun, adhere fabric to back side of sofa. Using fabric scissors, trim off excess fabric.

Back of Sofa Diagram

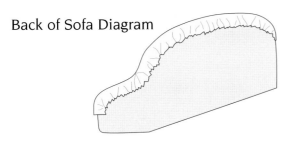

5. Temporarily fold fabric from front toward back. Place batting on seat cushions for extra "poof." Using hot-glue gun, dot-glue to secure.

6. Dot-glue at sofa center where batting meets the sofa back. Using your fingers, smooth fabric down sofa back and onto glue. Then work 1" areas at a time, alternating from one side of center to the other, toward outer corners of sofa, and over each arm to keep fabric tension controlled and even.

7. Apply a thin line of glue at center front under frame bottom. Using your fingers, smooth fabric over batting, down the front, and under frame onto glue. Then work 1" areas at a time from one side of center to the other, toward outer corners of sofa to keep fabric tension controlled and even across seat.

8. Return to corners and work to ends of arms, continuing to wrap around and adhere to back side of sofa. Allow glue to cool. Using fabric scissors, trim off excess fabric that was pulled to the back and under the sofa.

9. Lay sofa on its back on clean piece of paper. Make pattern for back by rolling sofa from the end of one arm, across back, and to the end of remaining arm. Using pencil, draw around shape.

10. Using craft scissors, cut out paper pattern. Wrap pattern around arms and back side of

sofa to check fit. Adjust pattern as necessary.

11. Using pencil, trace pattern onto cardboard. Using craft scissors, cut out. Using pencil, mark front and back of cardboard pattern.

12. Using craft scissors, trim ¼" off paper pattern all around. Pin trimmed pattern on batting. Using fabric scissors, cut out. Using hot-glue gun, dot-glue around edges of batting and adhere to front of cardboard shape.

13. Place a 5" x 10" piece of fabric, wrong side up, on work surface. Center and place cardboard shape, batting side down, on fabric. Using pencil, mark around cardboard shape, adding ½" all around. Using fabric scissors, cut out. Apply permanent liquid adhesive, 2"–3" at a time, along edge of cardboard shape and wrap fabric over onto glue. Continue gluing

and wrapping all around cardboard shape. Using your fingers, press to smooth around edges. Allow to dry.

14. Working quickly, apply a thin line of hot glue ⅛" from covered edges of cardboard shape. Center and adhere glued side of cardboard shape to back side of sofa. Using your fingers, press firmly from side to side.

15. Using measuring tape, measure around base of sofa, adding 1½", to determine length of braided fringe. Using fabric scissors, cut trim. Using hot-glue gun and beginning at center back side of sofa, adhere braided fringe around bottom of sofa, butting ends together, and allowing braid to skim floor.

16. Repeat Steps 1–15 for covering chair forms.

Linen roses: *decorator pillows*

SEE PHOTO ON PAGE 32.

YOU WILL NEED:
- Batting: fluffy
- Fabric: solid cotton; cotton with large floral print
- Fabric scissors

- Fusible liquid adhesive
- Iron and ironing board
- Pressing cloth

MAKING THE PROJECT:

1. Using fabric scissors, cut out a large fabric flower. Using cut-out flower as a pattern, cut a piece of solid cotton fabric for backing to match shape for pillow back.

2. Place flower, wrong side up, on work surface. Apply a thin line of fusible liquid adhesive around edges, leaving a ¾" opening. Adhere matching shape to flower and, using iron and pressing cloth, press to seal.

3. Stuff with batting. Apply a thin line of fusible liquid adhesive along one edge of opening and press to seal opening closed.

4. Repeat Steps 1–3 for desired number of pillows. Place pillows on sofa and chairs.

Fringed edges: *area rug*

YOU WILL NEED:
- Braid trim with tiny tassels: (1½ yd.)
- Hot-glue gun and glue sticks
- Precut carpet for dollhouses

MAKING THE PROJECT:

1. Place carpet, right side up, on work surface. Using hot-glue gun, apply glue, 2"–3" at a time, along one edge of carpet and adhere straight side of braid onto carpet so fringe is extending beyond carpet. Continue gluing braid all around edges. If desired, loop braid at corners.

Formal stripes: *table runner*

YOU WILL NEED:
- Fabric scissors
- Measuring tape
- Miniature dining room table

- Ribbon: 2"-wide, satin (10")

MAKING THE PROJECT:

1. Using measuring tape, measure tabletop length. Using fabric scissors, cut ribbon to this dimension.

2. Cut each corner off ribbon, making a point in the center at each short end.

3. Center and place runner on table.

Woven fibers: *hutch blanket*

You will need:
- Fabric: textured loose weave
- Fabric scissors
- Hot-glue gun and glue sticks
- Measuring tape
- Miniature hutch

Making the project:
1. Using measuring tape, measure hutch shelf's width and height.

2. Using fabric scissors, cut a long fabric strip to width dimension. Beginning at one end, roll strip to height dimension. Cut strip at this point.

3. Pull threads, one at a time, along exposed end to fringe edge about ½".

4. Using hot-glue gun, dot-glue end of roll to secure. Dot-glue bottom of roll and secure onto shelf.

Wainscotting: *wall decor & chair railing*

See photo on page 38.

You will need:
- Craft knife
- Fabric: damask (½ yd.)
- Fabric scissors
- Foam core board
- Gel stain
- Hot-glue gun and glue sticks
- Iron and ironing board
- Measuring tape
- Metal ruler
- Miter box and saw for miniatures
- Permanent liquid adhesive
- Rag
- Varnish for crafts
- Wood glue
- Wood molding: ½"-wide

Making the project:
1. Using iron on steam setting, press fabric.

2. Using measuring tape, measure back wall for width, adding 1". Measure from ceiling down two-thirds of the wall, adding 1". Using fabric scissors, cut fabric to those dimensions.

3. Subtract ¼" from total of each measurement and, using metal ruler, mark foam

core board to those dimensions. Using craft knife, cut out along markings.

4. Liberally and evenly apply permanent liquid adhesive to front of foam core board. Center and adhere fabric, right side up, onto foam core board. Using your fingers, smooth out any wrinkles in fabric.

5. Using fabric scissors, cut corners of fabric. Apply a thin line of permanent liquid adhesive along top back edge of foam core board. Wrap top edge of fabric over edge of foam core board and onto back. Allow to dry. Repeat for remaining edges. Trim fabric as necessary.

6. Using hot-glue gun, adhere back of fabric-covered foam core board onto wall at ceiling.

7. Using measuring tape, measure each side wall for height and width as in Step 2. Remember the width measurement begins at the fabric-covered foam core board on the back wall. Refer to Wall Covering Diagram. Cut fabric to those dimensions. Repeat Steps 3–6 for remaining walls.

Wall Covering Diagram

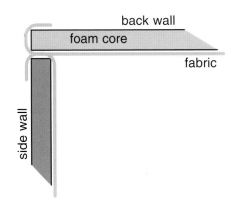

8. Using measuring tape, measure around doors and windows for molding, or width of wall where railing will be placed, adding 1" to total for margin of error.

9. Using miter box and saw for miniatures, straight-cut or miter-cut molding pieces, depending on where they will be placed, to dimensions determined in Step 8.

10. Check molding placement to make certain the doors are able to swing on their hinges. Trim molding as necessary.

11. Using a rag and following manufacturer's instructions, stain molding. Varnish molding.

12. Apply a small amount of wood glue to molding. Adhere molding onto walls just below fabric-covered foam core board or around doors and windows as desired. Refer to Molding Diagram. When placing both window molding and chair railing on the same wall, follow the visual line of the window's lower wood strip to create one continuous line that is pleasing to the eye.

Note: The center walls of some dollhouses may not be the same measurement as the side walls. Make certain to measure each wall carefully.

Molding Diagram

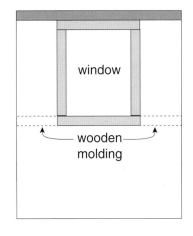

Austrian poof: *window treatment*

YOU WILL NEED:
- Acrylic paint: to match window
- Dowels: ⅛"-dia., ¾" longer than width of window (2)
- Fabric: crepe (8" x 10")
- Fabric scissors
- Fusible liquid adhesive
- Hot-glue gun and glue sticks
- Iron and ironing board
- Measuring tape
- Paintbrush: ¼" flat
- Pencil
- Pressing cloth
- Sewing needle and coordinating thread

MAKING THE PROJECT:

1. Using measuring tape, measure window height and width, doubling the width. Using fabric scissors, cut fabric to those dimensions.

2. Place fabric, wrong side up, on work surface. Apply a thin line of fusible liquid adhesive ⅛" from all edges. Fold each edge over ¼" and, using iron and pressing cloth, press to seal edges.

3. Using sewing needle and thread, gather-stitch from center bottom edge of fabric to ¾" down from top edge. Pull thread, gathering fabric to about 3" long and creating small pleats. Repeat gather-stitch along each side, ⅛" from edge.

4. Gather-stitch along top of fabric, ⅛" down from edge. Pull thread, gathering fabric to ¼" longer than length of dowels. Repeat gather-stitch along bottom edge.

5. Using paintbrush, paint dowels. Allow to dry.

6. Using pencil, mark center of dowels. Place gathered fabric, wrong side up and top edge closest to you, on work surface. Using hot-glue gun, dot-glue center mark on one dowel. Adhere center top edge of fabric to dowel.

7. Dot-glue one end of dowel. Wrap side top edge of fabric around end to back of dowel. Repeat for remaining end of dowel. Turn fabric over, right side up, on work surface. Evenly distribute gathers and dot-glue fabric to dowel from center point toward one end. Repeat in opposite direction.

8. Apply a dot of glue at center mark of remaining dowel. Adhere center of bottom edge of fabric to dowel. Apply a dot of glue to each end of dowel. Wrap and adhere side bottom edges of fabric around dowel ends to back of dowel. Allow fabric gathers to "drape."

9. Using hot-glue gun, dot-glue back of each end of top and bottom dowels. Adhere dowels to window frame.

Casual chic: *redecorating ideas*

Replace rich damask fabrics with soft cotton calicos and turn the formal living and dining room into a cozy and inviting area for more casual gatherings.

Above: *Divide a long piece of lightweight fabric into three equal sections. Tie a bow at each end of the center section with two pieces of narrow ribbon. Divide this section into three equal sections and tie a bow at each end of the center section. Evenly distribute gathers to create three draping sections. Adhere the back of the curtain to a dowel.*

Right: *Use colored papers to make tiny books for the bookshelf. Make book ends from sculpting clay. Add a fireplace and a bunch of flowers for the mantle.*

Above: Use lace-trimmed fabric pieces for curtains at each side of the window. Cover the tops of fabric pieces and window with a piece of lace.

Left: Paint the top third of walls with a light-colored acrylic paint. Paint remaining two-thirds of walls with a darker colored acrylic paint. Adhere a wide patterned ribbon to all walls, 1" down from the ceiling.

Garden Bathroom

powder

soaking tub

ceramic tile

basin

water closet

towels

porcelain

bathmat

soaps

private

bubblebath

bath beads

This botanical spa is the place for leaving behind the cares of the world and indulging in rest and relaxation.

The lattice wall design, topiary plants, and sunlight filtering through the sheer window shade bring the outdoors inside. The bath mat and braided rug are soft as the good earth underfoot. The air is alive with a gentle breeze moving through the trees, the sound of distant wind chimes, and the quiet trickle of a water fountain. The soothing lullaby of buzzing bees and singing birds can almost be heard.

Luxurious accessories—a bottle of rose water, bath salts, loufa sponges, and aromatherapy candles—are kept in the charming chest of drawers.

The raised porcelain tub is the perfect setting for a scented bubble bath—spending the evening eating fresh strawberries and reading the latest novel.

towels

bathmat

soaps

bubblebath

powder

Garden Bathroom

Soft pastels blend with the deep colors found in a rose garden to set the mood for this retreat. The wall behind the tub is mirrored to create the illusion of expansion.

Towels made of the fluffiest flannel are used as decorative details—rolled and tied together with a ribbon and placed in one corner, stacked near perfume bottles on the vanity table, and hung from the rack of an open cabinet holding lotions and soaps.

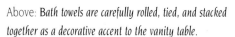

Above: Bath towels are carefully rolled, tied, and stacked together as a decorative accent to the vanity table.

Above right: A pretty little mat provides sure footing at the side of the bathtub.

Right: Hours can be spent bathing in the luxury of this room.

46

New-found flowers: *covered chest of drawers*

YOU WILL NEED:
- Corsage pin
- Fabric: cotton print
- Measuring tape
- Miniature chest with removable drawers
- Permanent liquid adhesive
- Small fabric scissors
- Straight-edge razor blade

MAKING THE PROJECT:

1. Using measuring tape, measure top and center core of chest and double the dimensions to determine necessary fabric yardage. Using small fabric scissors, cut fabric to those dimensions.

2. Remove drawers from chest and set aside. Using the head of corsage pin, dab permanent liquid adhesive evenly on chest surface. Wrap fabric around center core of chest. Using small fabric scissors, clip corner areas and wrap fabric to edges. Allow to dry. Using a straight-edge razor blade, cut out drawer spaces.

3. Using measuring tape, measure chest top and bottom, adding an adequate amount to wrap around edge plus ¼" more. Apply permanent liquid adhesive as in Step 2 and, using razor blade, trim excess fabric.

4. Wipe permanent liquid adhesive lightly over raw edges to avoid fraying. Allow to dry.

5. Using measuring tape, measure drawer front, adding ½" all around for wrapping around edges. Using small fabric scissors, cut fabric to those dimensions.

6. Position fabric over drawer and, using corsage pin, poke a small hole in fabric for each drawer handle to come through.

7. Apply permanent liquid adhesive as in Step 2 on drawer surface. Smooth fabric over surface. Using small fabric scissors, clip corners of fabric and wrap to edges. Allow to dry. Using razor blade, trim excess fabric.

8. Repeat Steps 5–7 for each drawer. Replace drawers.

Rags to riches: *circular braided rag rug*

YOU WILL NEED:
- Fabric: cotton, ½" x 45" strips (3)
- Fabric scissors
- Hot-glue gun and glue sticks
- Iron and ironing board
- Safety pin

MAKING THE PROJECT:

1. Fold and, using iron, press each fabric strip in half lengthwise to measure ¼" x 45".

2. Using hot-glue gun, adhere all three strips together at one end. Begin braiding strips at adhered end and continue until entire length is braided. Secure loose ends together with a safety pin.

3. Temporarily secure adhered end of braided strips to a flat surface. Begin winding braid clockwise around secured end into a circle. At regular intervals, adhere to secure edge to edge until all but 1"–2" of braid is wound and secured. Remove safety pin, unbraid, and, using fabric scissors, trim ends to ⅛" width. Braid trimmed ends and adhere to underside of rug. Remove from flat surface.

Note: A fabric backing, cut slightly smaller than the circumference of the rug, can be used to hide adhered edges.

Soft touch: *bath towels*

YOU WILL NEED:
- Appliqué: small rose
- Braid: ¼"-wide
- Fabric: flannel with very small pattern
- Fabric scissors
- Miniatures: dressing table; sink; towel rack; vanity stool
- Permanent liquid adhesive
- Ribbon: ⅛"-wide, satin for towel decor; 4mm, silk to tie towel rolls

MAKING THE PROJECT:

1. Using fabric scissors, cut flannel to desired sizes for bath towels, hand towels, and washcloths.

2. Apply permanent liquid adhesive to towels and adhere braid and satin ribbon as desired. Should fraying occur, turn fabric under ¼" on all edges.

3. Pull threads on two short ends to fringe edges about ⅛".

4. Dot center of bath towel with permanent liquid adhesive near braid and ribbon trim. Place rose appliqué onto adhesive. Finger-gather towel near the center. Dot folds with permanent liquid adhesive and adhere to vanity stool.

5. Roll three towels. Tie each with a length of silk ribbon. Clump rolled towels together and adhere with permanent liquid adhesive.

6. Fold one towel of each size in half. Stack towels on top of each other, largest to smallest, and adhere together with permanent liquid adhesive. Arrange grouping on one side of dressing table and adhere to table.

7. Fold two hand towels in half. Apply a line of permanent liquid adhesive along each fold and adhere one towel to each side of sink.

8. Center and place one hand towel on one bath towel and fold both lengthwise in half. Hang as one on towel rack.

Bath beads & baubles: *bath accessories*

SEE PHOTO ON PAGE 49.

YOU WILL NEED:
- Assorted jewelry pieces
- Hot-glue gun and glue sticks
- Pearl beads

MAKING THE PROJECT:
1. Using hot-glue gun, adhere stacked pearl beads and jewelry pieces together to resemble perfume bottles.

Soft & fluffy: *bath mat*

YOU WILL NEED:
- Batting: flat (1¼" x 1⅞")
- Braid: small (9")
- Fabric: coordinating cotton prints, 2" x 2¾" (2)
- Fusible liquid adhesive
- Iron and ironing board
- Permanent liquid adhesive
- Pressing cloth

MAKING THE PROJECT:
1. Place one print fabric, wrong side up, on work surface. Apply a thin line of fusible liquid adhesive ⅛" from all edges. Fold each edge over ¼" and, using iron and press-ing cloth, press to seal edges. Repeat for second print.

2. Apply a thin line of fusible liquid adhesive around all folded edges of first print fabric. Adhere braid onto fabric and press to seal.

3. Dot each corner of batting with permanent liquid adhesive. Center batting and adhere to wrong side of first print fabric.

4. Center second print fabric, right side up, over batting and braid. Apply a thin line of fusible liquid adhesive around all folded edges and press to seal edges.

Garden lattice: *wall design*

SEE PHOTOS ON PAGE 52.

YOU WILL NEED:
- Acrylic paint: to match decor
- Cardboard: thin (¾" x 4" strip)
- Craft knife
- Measuring tape
- Miter box and saw for miniatures
- Paintbrushes: ½" flat; 1" sponge
- Pencil
- Permanent liquid adhesive
- Ribbon: ⅛"-wide, satin, (1 spool)
- Scissors: craft; fabric
- Small metallic squares, or Mylar or mirror (6" square)
- Spray acrylic sealer
- Wood glue
- Wood molding: ½"-wide

MAKING THE PROJECT:

1. Using sponge paintbrush, apply two coats of paint to all walls and ceiling of bathroom. Allow to dry between coats.

2. Using measuring tape, measure width of walls where molding will be placed, adding 1" to total for margin of error.

3. Using flat paintbrush, apply two coats of paint to molding. Allow to dry between coats. Spray painted molding two to three times with spray acrylic sealer. Allow to dry between coats.

4. For molding, use miter box and saw for miniatures to straight-cut or miter-cut molding pieces, depending on where they will be placed, to dimensions determined in Step 2. Set pieces aside.

5. For lattice, measure from ceiling down on two walls. Using a pencil, mark a horizontal line along these walls to indicate where ribbon will stop and molding will start.

6. Using craft scissors, cut one end of cardboard strip to a 45° angle as shown in Ribbon Template Diagram.

Ribbon Template Diagram

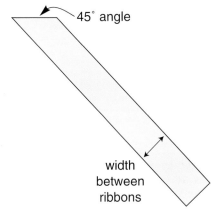

45° angle

width between ribbons

7. Position cardboard strip as a guide, with the 45° angle against ceiling. Using pencil, begin at one side of one wall and lightly draw a line along top edge of cardboard from ceiling to molding placement point. Mark along bottom edge of cardboard in same manner. Move top edge of cardboard to this last line and mark along bottom edge. Continue until width of both walls is marked.

8. Turn cardboard guide over and position 45° angle against ceiling. Reverse direction of pattern, using pencil and marking width of both walls as in Step 7.

9. Using fabric scissors, cut ribbon to length of angled pencil marks beginning at one end of one wall and running in one direction. Cut ribbon ends at a 45° angle.

10. Apply a thin line of permanent liquid adhesive along the wrong side of ribbon—one piece at a time. Adhere ribbon onto first line of one wall. Continue adhering ribbon around both walls in one direction, making certain it is adhering well to the wall. Allow ribbons to dry for an hour.

11. Adhere ribbons around both walls in opposite direction as in Step 10, overlapping previously placed ribbons.

12. Using craft knife, trim ribbon ends along pencil line indicating molding placement.

13. Check molding placement to make certain doors are able to open properly. Trim molding as necessary.

14. Apply small amount of wood glue to molding. Adhere molding onto walls, placing over ribbon ends, and around doors and windows as desired.

15. For reflective tiles, use measuring tape to measure from bottom of molding to floor, and width of miniature bathtub platform to determine amount of metallic squares, mylar, or mirror needed. Lay reflective material out, wrong side up, on work surface.

16. Apply wood glue to each piece of reflective material and adhere onto wall to fill area behind bathtub.

Rolled up: *window treatment*

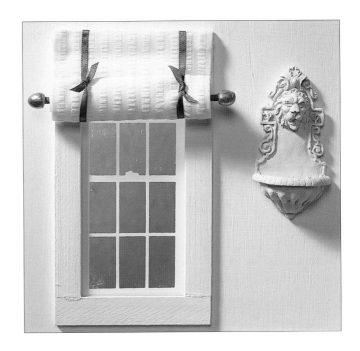

YOU WILL NEED:
- Acrylic paint: to match window
- Dowel: ⅛"-dia., ½" longer than width of window
- Fabric: cotton (3½" x 9")
- Fabric scissors
- Fusible liquid adhesive
- Hot-glue gun and glue sticks
- Iron and ironing board
- Paintbrush: ¼" flat
- Permanent liquid adhesive
- Pressing cloth
- Ribbon: ⅛"-wide, satin (18")
- Sculpting clay: coordinating color for dowel ball ends

MAKING THE PROJECT:

1. Using paintbrush, paint dowel. Allow to dry.

2. Roll a small bit of clay into two pea-sized balls. Poke each ball midway with one end of dowel. Remove dowel. Bake clay following manufacturer's instructions. Allow to cool.

3. Using hot-glue gun, adhere one clay ball to each end of dowel.

4. Place fabric, wrong side up, on work surface. Apply a thin line of fusible liquid adhesive ⅛" from long edges of fabric. Fold edges over ¼" and, using iron and pressing cloth, press to seal edges.

5. Apply a thin line of fusible liquid adhesive ⅛" from one short edge of fabric. Fold edge over ¼" and press to seal edges.

6. Turn fabric right side up. Apply a thin line of fusible liquid adhesive ⅛" from remaining short edge. Place sealed short edge onto glue, creating a tube, and press to seal.

7. Position seam at top of fabric tube. Using fabric scissors, cut ribbon into two equal pieces. Fold each piece of ribbon in half. Place fold of each ribbon at top, or seam, of fabric tube, ½" from each side edge. Apply a dot of permanent liquid adhesive at front and back of seam to adhere each ribbon in place.

8. Place fabric tube, front side up, on work surface. Insert dowel through tube and position it at bottom of tube. Using your fingers, smooth fabric flat.

9. Securing dowel ends, roll fabric up to 1½" from top. Apply dots of permanent liquid adhesive as necessary to keep fabric rolled.

10. Smooth each ribbon down back and front of rolled fabric, bringing each pair of ends together and knotting at front on top of roll to hold in place.

11. Using hot-glue gun, adhere wrong side of top of fabric to top of window frame.

Check out: *redecorating ideas*

Instead of a garden theme in the bathroom, try mixing neutral woven patterns with bold checks for an art deco scheme. Create depth and dimension by using contrasting accent colors.

Above: **Use a wide patterned ribbon to tie up a blind made from a solid-colored fabric.**

Right: **Loosely weave ribbon over a painted back wall. Use a wide patterned ribbon to edge floor tiles.**

54

Master Suite

canopy

armoire

pillow

vanity

bolster

sanctuary

afghan

chaise

nightstand

tassels

suite

comforter

Borrowing from an era when men were chivalrous and women were ladies, the master suite embodies all the romance, charm, and luxury of days gone by.

The day's activities begin and end in this place of peace and comfort. The morning breaks as the man of the house awakens and prepares to leave for the office. His wife rises and contemplates in front of the armoire how she should dress to accomplish the various duties of the day.

In the afternoon, she will take a break from housework to do something she loves—stretch out on the French chaise lounge and add a few new stitches to her needlepoint.

Evening will find her seated in a silk nightgown on the plush cushion of the vanity bench. She brushes her long silken tresses with a sterling silver hairbrush, preparing to retire to bed with her husband.

vanity

pillow

sanctuary

afghan

nightstand

Master Suite

Thoughtful details make the master suite a room with a view. A tasseled lamp and a small bouquet of lily of the valley sit on the bedside table, inviting the company of a book of poetry by Robert Browning.

Delicate lace and satiny ribbon accent the sheet and pillow cases on the four-poster canopy bed. A single red rose is placed on a lover's pillow, accompanied by a tiny love letter composed on fine parchment paper from the dressing table.

A plush crocheted afghan, flung over the footboard, is within reach for curling up in on the coolest of evenings.

The dusty blue found in the vanity seat cushion acts as an accent color to the warm surroundings of monochromatic whites and creamy yellows. Together, they set the stage for romantic ambience.

Left: *The dressing table is placed opposite the canopy bed so the contents of the room can be viewed from the mirror.*

Below: *A delicate red rose is placed on the bed to suggest that romance is alive and well.*

Elegant adornment: *lace canopy*

YOU WILL NEED:
- Fabric: lace (12" square); 6"-wide, tulle (2 yds.)
- Fabric scissors
- Hot-glue gun and glue sticks
- Measuring tape
- Miniature canopy bed
- Permanent liquid adhesive
- Ribbon: ¼"-wide, satin (1 yd.)
- Sewing needle and coordinating thread
- Straight-edge razor blade

MAKING THE PROJECT:

1. Using straight-edge razor blade, remove any existing fabrics from canopy and bed frame.

2. Using measuring tape, determine length by measuring from front edge of frame above footboard, up, and over curve, and continuing to back edge above headboard. Measure width of frame. Using fabric scissors, cut lace to those dimensions.

3. Using hot-glue gun, dot-glue across canopy frame above headboard. Quickly adhere short edge of lace onto frame.

4. Dot-glue along top of one long side of canopy frame. Quickly adhere corresponding long edge of lace onto frame. Repeat for remaining side and short end above footboard, smoothing lace as you go. Using razor blade, trim excess all around.

5. Using fabric scissors, cut tulle into 1"-wide strips. Using sewing needle and thread, gather-stitch ⅛" from one long edge of each strip, shirring and whipping to secure pieces together. Feed strips onto needle, one after another, until there are enough to go on each side of canopy and across bottom.

6. Using hot-glue gun, adhere the long shirred tulle onto canopy frame from one top post, along one side, along end above the footboard, along the remaining side, and up to the remaining top post.

7. Using fabric scissors, cut ribbon to cover raw edges of tulle around top edge of canopy frame. Apply a thin line of permanent liquid adhesive along top edge of frame between posts and adhere ribbon onto frame.

Victorian detail: *shirred headboard*

YOU WILL NEED:
- Fabric: crepe (¼ yd.)
- Fabric scissors
- Hot-glue gun and glue sticks
- Iron and ironing board
- Measuring tape
- Miniature canopy bed
- Sewing needle and coordinating thread

MAKING THE PROJECT:

1. Using measuring tape, determine width by measuring across canopy frame above headboard and double measurement. Measure from top edge of canopy frame to bottom of headboard frame along outside of the bed. Using fabric scissors, cut fabric to those dimensions.

2. Fold one long edge of fabric under ¼". Using

iron, press fold. Using sewing needle and thread, gather-stitch ⅛" from fold to equal width of bed and canopy frame. Fold side raw edges under and, using iron, press to fold. Hold gathered fabric up to top edge of canopy frame and mark for length where it will be adhered onto bottom edge of headboard. Fold fabric at mark and, using iron, press fold. Gather-stitch along folded bottom edge to same width as top.

3. Using hot-glue gun, dot-glue across top of canopy frame. Adhere right side of fabric at top gathered end onto canopy frame. Allow to cool. Gently stretch fabric toward bottom edge of headboard, equally distributing the shirring. Adhere bottom gathered edge of fabric onto bottom of headboard.

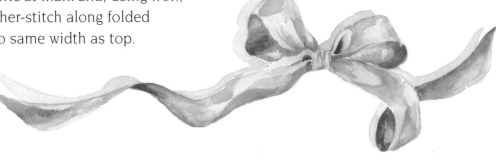

Tucked away: *bottom sheet*

See photo on page 63.

You will need:
- Fabric: cotton (12" square)
- Fabric scissors
- Fusible liquid adhesive
- Hot-glue gun and glue sticks
- Iron and ironing board
- Measuring tape
- Miniature canopy bed
- Pins
- Pressing cloth
- Straight-edge razor blade

Making the project:
1. Using straight-edge razor blade, remove any existing fabrics from mattress.

2. Using measuring tape, measure from bottom of bed frame on one side to top of mattress, across mattress, and down other side to bottom of bed frame. Measure from headboard to footboard, adding ½". Using fabric scissors, cut fabric to those dimensions.

3. Place fabric, wrong side up, on work surface. Apply a thin line of fusible liquid adhesive ⅛" from both long edges. Fold each edge over ¼" and, using iron and pressing cloth, press to seal edges.

4. Fold top and bottom edges of fabric over ¼" and press fold.

5. Fold fabric in half lengthwise, with sealed edges together. Pin at each end to mark center. Unfold fabric. Using measuring tape, measure width of mattress near headboard and footboard and pin at each end to mark center. Place center of fabric top and bottom on center of mattress top and bottom. Remove all pins. Wrap fabric firmly from center around to one side of bed. Using hot-glue gun, adhere wrapped edge along bottom of bed frame.

6. Smooth fabric across mattress and wrap remaining edge over other side of bed. Adhere wrapped edge along bottom of bed frame.

7. Using a thin smooth object, tuck top and bottom of "sheet" in between mattress and headboard and footboard to hide raw edges.

Pretty percale: *top sheet*

YOU WILL NEED:
- Fabric: cotton (12" square)
- Fabric scissors
- Fusible liquid adhesive
- Iron and ironing board
- Lace trim: ¼"-wide with scalloped edge
- Measuring tape
- Miniature canopy bed
- Ribbon: ¼"-wide, satin
- Pressing cloth

MAKING THE PROJECT:

1. Using measuring tape, measure from floor, up one side of bed, across width of mattress, and down other side to floor. Measure length of mattress, adding 2". Using fabric scissors, cut fabric to those dimensions.

2. Place fabric, wrong side up, on work surface. Apply a thin line of fusible liquid adhesive ⅛" from bottom and side edges. Fold each edge over ¼" and, using iron and pressing cloth, press to seal edges. Apply a thin line of fusible liquid adhesive ⅛" from top edge. Fold edge over ¼" and press to seal.

3. Using fabric scissors, cut lace trim to width of fabric. Place fabric, wrong side up, on work surface. Apply a thin line of fusible liquid adhesive ⅛" from top edge of "sheet." Adhere straight edge of lace, wrong side up, onto top edge of fabric. Using iron and pressing cloth, press to seal edges.

4. Using fabric scissors, cut satin ribbon slightly longer than the width of fabric. Place fabric, right side up, on work surface. Apply a thin line of fusible liquid adhesive ¼" from top edge of fabric. Center and adhere wrong side of satin ribbon onto fabric. Using iron and pressing cloth, press to seal. Fold ribbon ends under and press to secure.

Proper headrest: *bed pillows*

Making the project:

1. Using fabric scissors, cut two 6" x 3½" pieces of fabric. Place fabric pieces, wrong side up, on work surface. Apply a thin line of fusible liquid adhesive ⅛" from long edges of each piece. Fold each edge over ¼" and, using iron and pressing cloth, press to seal edges. Apply a thin line of fusible liquid adhesive along short edges. Fold edges over ¼" and press to seal.

2. Using fabric scissors, cut two pieces of lace trim to width of fabric for each pillow. Apply a thin line of fusible liquid adhesive ⅛" from each folded short edge of fabric. Adhere straight edge of lace, wrong side up, onto fabric. Using iron and pressing cloth, press to seal.

3. Using fabric scissors, cut satin ribbon slightly longer than width of fabric. Place fabric, right side up, on work surface. Apply a thin line of fusible liquid adhesive ⅛" from short edges of fabric. Center and adhere wrong side of satin ribbon onto fabric. Using iron and pressing cloth, press to seal. Fold ribbon ends under and press to secure.

4. Fold each fabric piece, wrong sides together, so short laced edges meet. Apply a thin line of fusible liquid adhesive along long inside edges. Press to seal edges. Allow to cool.

5. Stuff with fluffy batting. If desired, apply a thin line of fusible liquid adhesive inside opening. Press to seal opening closed.

Beauty in damask: *bedspread*

SEE PHOTO ON PAGE 65.

YOU WILL NEED:
- Batting: flat (12" square)
- Fabric: damask (12" square); cotton print (12" square)
- Fabric scissors
- Fusible liquid adhesive
- Iron and ironing board
- Measuring tape
- Pins
- Pressing cloth

MAKING THE PROJECT:

1. Using measuring tape, measure from floor, up one side of bed, across width of mattress, and down other side to floor. Measure length of mattress, adding ¼". Using fabric scissors, cut both damask fabric and cotton fabric to those dimensions.

2. Place damask fabric, wrong side up, on work surface. Apply a thin line of fusible liquid adhesive ⅛" from all edges. Fold each edge over ¼" and, using iron and pressing cloth, press to seal edges. Pin to mark top edge of fabric. Repeat for cotton fabric.

3. Using fabric scissors, cut batting ¼" smaller than damask fabric all around.

4. Center and place batting on wrong side of cotton fabric. Apply a thin line of fusible liquid adhesive ⅛" from top and both side edges of cotton fabric. Center and place damask fabric, right side up, on batting. Using iron and pressing cloth, press to seal edges.

5. Place spread on mattress with open end at footboard and equal amounts of fabric hanging over each side of bed. Pin to mark spread at footboard just within each bed post. Using measuring tape, measure between bed posts at footboard, adding ½". Measure from top of mattress at footboard to floor adding ½". Using fabric scissors, cut damask fabric, cotton fabric, and batting to those dimensions. Trim batting ½" on one short edge.

6. Place damask fabric, wrong side up, on work surface. Apply a thin line of fusible liquid adhesive ⅛" from all edges of each fabric. Fold each edge over ¼" and, using iron and pressing cloth, press to seal edges. Repeat for cotton fabric.

7. Center and place batting on wrong side of cotton fabric. Apply a thin line of fusible liquid adhesive ⅛" from all edges of lining fabric. Center and place damask fabric, right side up, on batting. Press to seal edges, creating a flap.

8. Remove spread from bed. Apply a thin line of fusible liquid adhesive inside opening from each side seam to pin. Press to seal opening closed.

9. Place spread, damask side up, on work surface. Insert ½" of flap, damask side up, into spread to fit opening.

10. Apply a thin line of fusible liquid adhesive along damask and cotton inside edges of spread opening. Press to seal flap within spread.

Frame embellishment: *bedpost tassels*

YOU WILL NEED:
- Cardboard: thin (1" square)
- Embroidery floss
- Embroidery needle
- Miniature canopy bed with spread
- Scissors: craft; fabric

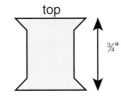

MAKING THE PROJECT:

1. Using craft scissors and Tassel Pattern, cut cardboard pattern.

Tassel Pattern

top

¾"

2. Using fabric scissors, cut a 4" piece of floss. Center floss on cardboard lengthwise so floss extends beyond top and bottom of cardboard.

3. Cut an 8" piece of floss. Holding 4" piece of floss in place, wind 8" piece of floss around cardboard from side to side, moving from top to bottom. Take up ends of 4" piece of floss and tie in a tight knot at top of cardboard, bringing all floss loops together. Gently squeeze cardboard so floss slides off. Place looped floss on work surface.

4. Cut a 6" piece of floss. Wind 6" piece around looped floss a third of the way down from one looped end, two to three times, and tie in tight knot at back. Cut loops at long end to create tassel. Fluff tassel ends.

5. Thread needle with 12" of floss. Take needle through bed spread flap at one corner behind bed post, removing needle and leaving two 6" strands attached to corner. Repeat for remaining corner of bed spread.

6. Criss-cross floss around each bed post two to three times and knot at underside of spread. Tie completed tassel to bed post.

Fancy reflection: *oval mirror*

YOU WILL NEED:
- Batting: flat (4" square)
- Cameo (optional)
- Cardboard: 6" square
- Fabric: cotton 3" square (2); tulle (3" square)
- Hot-glue gun and glue sticks
- Oval mirror: 2" x 1"
- Pencil
- Ribbon: ¾"-wide, wired (15")
- Scissors: craft; fabric
- White paper

MAKING THE PROJECT:

1. Enlarge Oval Mirror Pattern. Using pencil, trace outer line onto white paper. Using craft scissors, cut out oval pattern.

2. Place oval pattern on cardboard. Using pencil, trace two ovals. Using craft scissors, cut out cardboard ovals.

3. Place one cardboard oval on each cotton fabric. Using fabric scissors, cut fabric out around cardboard oval, adding ¾" all around. Repeat for tulle.

4. Using craft scissors, cut center oval out of one cardboard oval. Place cardboard oval on batting. Using fabric scissors, cut batting around cardboard oval. Cut center oval out of batting.

5. Using hot-glue gun, adhere batting onto cardboard oval with cut-out center.

6. Center and place one cotton oval and tulle oval as one, right side up, on batting. Turn all pieces over as one so fabric is right side down on work surface. Using fabric scissors, cut an "X" in center of fabric. With length of oval running top to bottom, cut from center to top of center oval, center to bottom of center oval, and center to each side of center oval. Snip between each of these cuts within center oval.

7. Using hot-glue gun, dot-glue around center oval on back side of cardboard oval. Pull fabric slices through center oval and adhere onto back side of cardboard oval, beginning at top, then bottom, and alternating opposite slices all around. Work carefully, smoothing fabric as you go.

8. Using fabric scissors, cut all around outside edge of fabric, ¼" from edge. Using hot-glue gun, adhere fabric onto back side of cardboard oval, beginning at top, then bottom, and alternating opposite slices all around, creating a puffy oval.

9. Place remaining cotton oval, wrong side up, on work surface. Center remaining cardboard oval, wrong side up, on cotton oval. Using fabric scissors, cut all around outside edge of fabric, ¼" from edge. Using hot-glue gun, dot-glue wrong side of cardboard oval and adhere fabric, beginning at top, then bottom, and alternating opposite slices all around.

10. Apply a thin line of glue all around edge of wrong side of fabric-covered oval. Adhere wrong side of puffy oval onto fabric-covered oval.

11. Push mirror tightly into center of puffy oval for placement. Remove mirror and apply a thin line of glue on back side of mirror ⅛" from edge. Adhere mirror into puffy oval, holding it in place until secure.

12. If desired, apply a dot of glue to center of mirror. Center and adhere cameo onto mirror.

13. Apply a dot of glue to center top on back side of oval. Adhere one end of 4" piece of wired ribbon onto oval. Tie a multi-looped bow in remaining end of ribbon. Apply a dot of glue to back side of bow and adhere onto wall.

Oval Mirror Pattern
Enlarge 120%

Tiny stitches: *embroidery hoop*

SEE PHOTO ON PAGE 68.

YOU WILL NEED:
- Adjustable toy rings (2)
- Belfast linen 32 ct. (3" square)
- Embroidery needle and DMC floss
- Fabric scissors

MAKING THE PROJECT:

1. Using embroidery needle and floss, center and stitch motif on linen.

2. Adjust one ring so it fits inside the other. Place motif between rings as if in an embroidery hoop. Using fabric scissors, trim linen to 1½" square.

Step 1: Cross-stitch (1 strand)

666 Christmas Red–bright
701 Christmas Green–lt.

Step 2: Backstitch (1 strand)

701 Christmas Green–lt.

Buttoned up: *decorator pillow on lounge*

SEE PHOTO ON PAGE 68.

YOU WILL NEED:
- Batting: fluffy
- Button: ¼" dia., pearl with two holes (1)
- Fabric: crepe (4"); lace (4")
- Fabric scissors
- Pins
- Sewing needle and coordinating thread

MAKING THE PROJECT:

1. Place crepe and lace fabric squares together as one, with wrong side of lace to right side of crepe fabric. Pin to secure. Using fabric scissors, cut pinned fabrics into a 3½"-dia. circle.

2. Using sewing needle and thread, gather-stich ⅛" from edge around circle.

3. Pull threads to gather the circle, cupping fabric. Fill gathered circle with batting until very puffy. Draw thread tight and whip to secure. Center cinched area for back of pillow.

4. Insert needle into pillow at cinched area and bring it out at the center of the pillow front. Take needle up through one hole of small button. Push button firmly into center of pillow and take needle down through remaining hole of button, through pillow, bringing it out at cinched area.

5. Repeat Step 4. Whip thread at pillow back to secure.

Quiet mood: *lamp shade*

SEE PHOTO ON PAGE 68.

YOU WILL NEED:
- Braid trim with tiny tassels: (12")
- Fabric scissors
- Miniature table lamp with silk lamp shade
- Permanent liquid adhesive

MAKING THE PROJECT:

1. Using fabric scissors, cut tassels off braid.

2. Apply a thin line of permanent liquid adhesive around bottom edge of silk lamp shade. Adhere tassels onto shade.

Luxurious wrap: *afghan*

YOU WILL NEED:
- Crochet hook
- Fabric scissors
- Knitting needles: size 8
- Yarn: nubby bouchlé or mohair (1 skein)

MAKING THE PROJECT:

1. Refer to a knitting instruction book. Using knitting needles, cast on 14 stitches. Knit each row until length is 7". Cast off.

2. Using fabric scissors, cut 30 pieces of yarn 3" long for fringe. Refer to Hooking Diagram. Insert crochet hook through each set of cast-on stitches. Fold cut piece of yarn in half and pull loop through the set of two stitches. Using your fingers, work the two cut yarn ends through loop and pull ends tightly to create a fringe. Repeat for cast off stitches.

3. Using fabric scissors, trim fringe evenly on both ends of afghan.

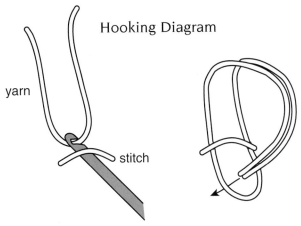

Hooking Diagram

yarn

stitch

Eye-pleasing partitions: *fabric-covered walls*

YOU WILL NEED:
- Craft knife
- Fabric: damask (½ yd.)
- Foam core board: (1 sheet)
- Hot-glue gun and glue sticks
- Iron and ironing board
- Measuring tape
- Metal ruler
- Pencil
- Permanent liquid adhesive

MAKING THE PROJECT:

1. Using iron set for steam, press fabric. (If using dark color, press wrong side.)

2. Using measuring tape, measure height and width of back wall, adding ½" to each measurement. Cut fabric to those dimensions.

3. Subtract ¼" from total of each measurement and, using ruler, mark foam core board to those dimensions. Using craft knife, cut out foam core along markings.

4. Liberally and evenly apply permanent liquid adhesive to front of foam core board. Center and adhere fabric, right side up, onto foam core board. Using your fingers, smooth out any wrinkles in fabric.

5. Using fabric scissors, clip corners of fabric. Apply a thin line of permanent liquid adhesive along top edge of foam core board. Wrap fabric over edge to back of foam core board. Repeat for remaining edges. Trim edges as necessary.

6. Using hot-glue gun, adhere back side of fabric-covered foam core board onto wall.

7. Using measuring tape, measure each side wall for height and width. Refer to Wall Covering Diagram. Remember width measurement begins at fabric-covered foam core board on back wall. Cut fabric to those dimensions. Repeat Steps 3–6 for remaining walls.

Wall Covering Diagram

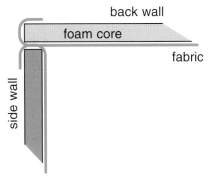

- back wall
- foam core
- fabric
- side wall

Note: The center walls of some doll houses do not have the same extending measurements and, therefore, do not match the side walls in inches. Measure each wall carefully.

Touch of brass: *window treatment*

YOU WILL NEED:
- Braid trim: twice the length of window
- Fabric: lace (one repeat per window) with finished lace edge
- Fabric scissors
- Filigree motifs: gold (2 for each window)
- Hot-glue gun and glue sticks
- Measuring tape
- Permanent liquid adhesive

MAKING THE PROJECT:

1. Using measuring tape, measure width of window from one outer edge of window frame to opposite outer edge. Measure height of window from top of frame to just below lock on window.

2. Using fabric scissors, cut lace fabric to dimensions in Step 1 so finished lace edge will be at top and bottom of window treatment.

3. Cut braid trim into two equal pieces. Apply a thin line of permanent liquid adhesive along both raw side edges of lace fabric. Adhere each piece of braid trim onto fabric.

4. Using hot-glue gun, adhere top edge of completed window treatment onto top of window frame. Allow to cool.

5. Adhere filigree motifs onto wall at each upper corner or window treatment.

Quilt of generations: *redecorating ideas*

The master bedroom can take on a more relaxed atmosphere by replacing the Victorian decor with tiny antiques, painted furniture, and heirloom quilts, afghans, and table runners.

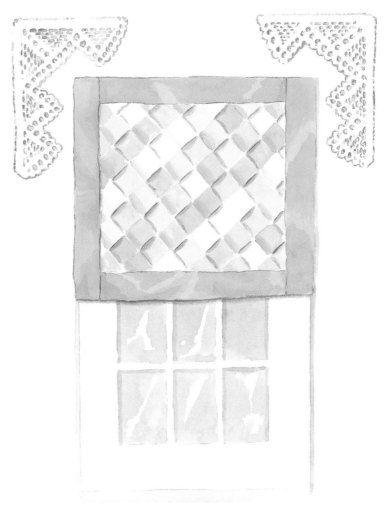

Above: *Weave several different colored ribbons to form a blind to match bedspread. Bind edges with one colored ribbon.*

Right: *Knit a multicolored afghan from yarn remnants. Stencil furniture and paint drawer handles to match. Make dressing table runner from wide ribbon.*

Sewing
Room

Mother is an inspiration with her unique way of teaching the children. Instead of shooing them outside to play, she keeps them with her in the creative atmosphere of the sewing room. They are kept busy cutting and piecing clothes together for their dolls.

There are three sewing machines in her room where, amidst the clutter, everything is in its place. At least one of these machines—worth its weight in gold—is always in use, stitching a fabulous silk or satin dress for the bride, the bride's maids, or her mother.

The hatbox holds the latest chapeau. Just a bit of organza or tulle makes up the perfect bridal veil. Treasures—jewels of special yardage, colorful trims, and patterned bolts of fabric—wait upon shelves, in shoeboxes, and in steamer trunks for the magic moment when they will be transformed into a gown that will be cherished and kept as an heirloom.

trims

patterns

notions

fabric bolts

pins

tailor

buttons

thimble

lace

lace
patterns
buttons
needles
scissors

Sewing Room

The many trims and fabrics of different colors and patterns, sitting on shelves and spilling out of a trunk, emphasize the busy nature of this room.

The organized clutter evokes memories of time spent in handmade pursuits. Paper patterns are tacked onto a pretty piece of fabric and laid on the cutting table—a project in process.

A full length mirror is strategically placed in the corner so everything in the room can been seen at once.

Above: *Two straight pins serve as knitting needles stuck into tiny yarn balls rolled from yarn remnants.*

Left: *Filled to overflowing, this room bustles with creativity as well as industry.*

Below: *A tiny hat box is tied with a smart gold and blue ribbon.*

Natty notions: *fabric & trims in cupboard*

YOU WILL NEED:
- Cardboard: lightweight
- Fabric: scraps
- Measuring tape
- Permanent liquid adhesive
- Scissors: craft; fabric
- Tiny trims: braid; lace; ribbon

MAKING THE PROJECT:

1. Using measuring tape, measure cupboard size to determine cut fabric sizes. (The samples shown use the given dimensions.)

2. Using fabric scissors, cut several fabric pieces 1½" x 2". Fray one long edge of each fabric piece by pulling threads along edge. Fold short sides of each fabric piece to

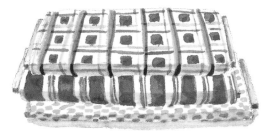

center so fabric measures 1½" x 1". Apply a dot of permanent liquid adhesive to adhere folds.

3. Fold each fabric so frayed edges are visible. Apply a dot of permanent liquid adhesive to adhere the two pieces together. Stack fabric on fabric shelf.

4. Continue stacking various colors and textures. Apply permanent liquid adhesive to adhere fabrics together so they are a comfortable height for each shelf they will be placed on.

5. For trims, refer to Tassel Pattern on page 67. Using craft scissors, cut several patterns from lightweight cardboard.

6. Apply a dot of permanent liquid adhesive on one end of cardboard pattern and adhere one tiny trim at a time. Wrap each trim three times around cardboard. Using fabric scissors, cut trim. Apply a dot of permanent liquid adhesive to adhere trim end in place. Each cardboard pattern should accommodate 2–3 different trims. Place on cupboard shelf, slightly tilted.

Textile treasures: *fabric rolls*

YOU WILL NEED:
- Dowels: ³⁄₁₆"-dia., 4½" long
- Fabric: various weights and textures
- Fabric scissors
- Hot-glue gun and glue sticks
- Ribbon: ⅛"-wide, contrasting color

MAKING THE PROJECT:
1. Using fabric scissors, cut various weights and textures of fabrics to 3½" x 4" each.

2. Using hot-glue gun, center and adhere one 4" edge of fabric piece onto dowel.

3. Roll fabric on dowel and dot-glue remaining edge onto rolled fabric.

4. Tie fabric with ribbon.

Storage solution: *suede trunk*

YOU WILL NEED:
- Fabric: ultra-suede, large enough to cover trunk
- Fabric chalk
- Fabric scissors
- Miniature trunk
- Permanent liquid adhesive
- Straight-edge razor blade

MAKING THE PROJECT:

1. Place trunk on its back at one straight edge of ultra-suede. Using chalk, mark slightly beyond top and bottom edges of trunk. Roll trunk from back to one side, to front, to remaining side, and to back again across suede, marking each edge as before. Using fabric scissors, cut at chalk line.

2. Liberally apply permanent liquid adhesive to outside of trunk and adhere suede to each matching side. Allow to dry. Using straight-edge razor blade, trim fabric closely along upper and lower edges for a clean line all around.

Scraps & snips: *cutting table*

You will need:
- Charms: scissors; rulers
- Fabric: cotton (10" square)
- Permanent liquid adhesive
- Scissors: craft; fabric
- Tissue paper

Making the project:

1. Using fabric scissors, cut fabric to 5" x 8½".

2. Fold fabric in half lengthwise. Place on table with ends hanging over each edge.

3. Choose desired pattern shapes, such as skirt and bodice patterns. Using craft scissors, cut shapes from tissue paper.

4. Apply a dot of permanent liquid adhesive to adhere patterns onto fabric on cutting table.

5. Place scissors or ruler charms on the table to make the setting even more authentic.

Ribboned cluster: *hat boxes*

SEE PHOTO ON OPPOSITE PAGE.

YOU WILL NEED:
- Hot-glue gun and glue sticks
- Miniature hat boxes (2)
- Pencil
- Ribbon: ⅜"-wide, wired (1 yd.)

MAKING THE PROJECT:

1. Using hot-glue gun, adhere bottom of one hat box to top of another hat box.

2. Fold ribbon in half to find center. Adhere center of ribbon under bottom box. Wrap ribbon tails up to top of boxes and tie as desired. Wrap tails around a pencil to curl ends.

Sitting pretty: *small stool*

YOU WILL NEED:
- Fabric: sheer lace or tulle
- Fabric scissors
- Hot-glue gun and glue sticks
- Measuring tape
- Miniature four-legged stool
- Ribbon: 2"-wide (¼ yd.)
- Satin rosette

Note: 6"-wide tulle on spools sold in crafts stores' bridal departments will work well for this project.

MAKING THE PROJECT:

1. Using measuring tape, measure height of stool and around legs at widest area. Double height measurement and add ½" to width measurement. Using fabric scissors, cut sheer fabric to those dimensions.

2. Fold fabric in half lengthwise and, using iron on medium heat setting, press fold.

3. Place raw edges of fabric at bottom edge of stool seat. Using hot-glue gun, adhere one end of fabric along one stool leg. Allow to cool. Wrap fabric around stool and adhere to each leg, slightly overlapping ends. Using fabric scissors, trim excess fabric.

4. Using fabric scissors, cut ribbon length to circumference of stool seat. Fold ribbon over ¾" lengthwise. Using hot-glue gun, adhere fold of ribbon around bottom edge of stool seat. Fold ribbon ends up diagonally and dot-glue to secure. Adhere rosette onto top of folded ribbon ends.

Couturère: *pedestal & draped mannequin*

YOU WILL NEED:
- Bowl: large, 2 qt.
- Dowel: 1¼"-dia., 1" long
- Fabric: cotton print (5" square); silk (3" x 18")
- Fabric scissors
- Fabric stiffening medium
- Hot-glue gun and glue sticks
- Iron and ironing board
- Ribbon: 1"-wide, satin (10")
- Rosette: silk
- Waxed paper

MAKING THE PROJECT:

1. For pedestal, using fabric scissors, cut 4½"-dia. circle from cotton. Pour fabric stiffening medium into bowl. Place cotton circle in medium, stirring to thoroughly coat.

2. Gently remove cotton circle from bowl, drawing it through your fingers to squeeze out excess medium.

3. Place cotton circle, wrong side up, on work surface covered with waxed paper. Fold cotton circle over ¼" around edge and finger-press to secure "hem" in place.

4. Center and place one end of dowel on cotton circle. Turn cotton circle and dowel right side up as one and place on work surface, allowing cotton to fall to waxed paper. Using your fingers, arrange folds of cotton and hemline, allowing to puddle all around table. Allow outside to dry. Turn upside down and allow inside to dry.

5. For draped mannequin, fold edges of silk over ¼" on each edge and, using iron, press folds. Using hot-glue gun, adhere one corner of one short edge at back of left shoulder and other corner at back of right waist on dress form. Bunch up silk around waist and adhere to secure.

6. Wrap silk down behind lower half of dress form. Loop silk upward, wrap around waist from left side to right, upward behind back, and above shoulder. Loop down to waist and up into back, hiding the end within the loops. Adhere silk to secure at every loop.

7. Place center of ribbon at back waist of dress form, wrap tails to front, and knot. Loop one tail, making a 1" loop. Adhere loop at knot. Loop ribbon again and adhere end of tail under second loop.

8. Using fabric scissors, cut remaining ribbon tail in a "V."

9. Using hot-glue gun, adhere silk rosette over knot in satin ribbon.

Creative retreat: *window treatment*

2. Using fabric scissors, cut lace twice the length of dowel for each window.

3. Place a glass pie dish upside down on work surface. Saturate lace with fabric stiffening spray. Place wet lace on dish bottom and finger-gather at regular intervals, referring to dowel length and allowing for yarn finials. Place dish with lace into microwave oven. Turn on microwave for 30 seconds or until lace is dry.

4. Using embroidery scissors, cut a ¼" slot in each dry gather along top edge. Thread painted dowel through gathers.

5. Using fabric scissors, cut yarn into two equal pieces. Using hot-glue gun, adhere one end of one piece of yarn to one dowel end. Wind yarn around dowel end as if winding a ball of yarn until ball is desired size. End winding on back side and dot-glue to secure. Repeat for remaining piece of yarn and dowel end.

6. Adhere dowel to top of window frame.

YOU WILL NEED:
- Acrylic paint: to match lace
- Dowel: ⅛"-dia., 1" longer than width of window
- Fabric stiffening spray
- Glass pie dish
- Hot-glue gun and glue sticks
- Lace: 2½"-wide, with scalloped/finished edges
- Microwave oven
- Paintbrush: ¼" flat
- Scissors: embroidery; fabric
- Silky yarn: remnant for rod ends

MAKING THE PROJECT:
1. Using paintbrush, paint dowel. Allow to dry.

Creativity prevails: *redecorating ideas*

Customize this room to reflect any creative outlet by decorating with related items, such as sketches, books, or an easel for an art room.

Above: **Pin tops of curtains above window frame and knot drapes to tie back.**

Left: **Decorate the art table with pencils made from the ends of colored toothpicks. Roll strips of colored papers and place in a fabric-covered trunk. Use a miniature garden ornament for a model and drape a length of fabric around it.**

Pretty-n-pink Nursery

rocker

bunting

mobile

pacifier

bassinet

canopy

lullaby

powder

fairy tale

nap time

dreams

A sweet baby girl is welcomed into the world with a nursery that expresses what little girls are made of.

The smell of baby powder is the scent of this special domain. The child begins life in this precious place as the princess of a kingdom called "home."

Mother sits in the rocking chair—a cherished heirloom given new life with a fresh coat of paint—gently rocking and singing the tired little one to sleep.

The stages of infanthood take place here as she learns to sit, then to crawl, and finally to toddle on her own two feet as she is coaxed forward by loving parents.

The interlude from newborn to toddler is too brief. She is experiencing the world, leaving behind this castle that her parents built for her. She sits on her tricycle for the first time as Father places her tiny feet on the pedals and sets her on the road to other kingdoms.

Pretty-n-pink Nursery

Soft comforting linens in coordinating colors and patterns—so nice to the touch—are placed with tender loving care.

Everything is clean and fresh. Colors are soft. Tones are quiet. What newborn would not wake up in this sweet room in a happy mood?

The decor is gentle and encompassing. The thoughtful placement of cushions, comforters, and quilts are just a few elements that ensure stimulation and security for the infant.

Above: *The floral comforter is pulled back to reveal the pink and blue polk-a-dot sheet on the crib mattress.*

Right: *The nursery is the perfect blend of both stimulation and serenity that are each essential for a baby's well-being.*

Satin rosebuds: *crib canopy*

SEE PHOTO ON PAGES 88–89.

YOU WILL NEED:
- Fabric: cotton, white
- Fabric scissors
- Fusible liquid adhesive
- Handkerchief: white with scallop edges
- Hot-glue gun and glue sticks
- Iron and ironing board
- Lace: 1½"-wide, eyelet with a decorative edge on one side (12–15")
- Measuring tape
- Miniature crib with canopy
- Pencil
- Permanent liquid adhesive
- Pins
- Satin rosebuds
- Straight-edge razor blade

MAKING THE PROJECT:

1. Using straight-edge razor blade, remove any existing fabric from canopy.

2. Using measuring tape, measure around canopy frame, adding 1". Using fabric scissors, cut lace to those dimensions.

3. Place lace, wrong side up, on work surface. Apply a thin line of permanent liquid adhesive along short edges and fold each edge over ⅛" for finished edges.

4. Using hot-glue gun, dot-glue along wrong side of straight edge of lace. Beginning at one back post, adhere one end of lace to side of canopy frame. Adhere lace along canopy frame back, one end, front, and remaining end, following the curve of the frame and ending at back post where lace began. Overlap remaining end of lace and dot-glue to secure.

5. Using razor blade, trim off any excess lace so it is flush with the top of canopy frame.

6. Using fabric scissors, cut fabric to exact dimensions of top of canopy frame. Cut out center of handkerchief to inside edge of scalloped edging, leaving scalloped edging intact. Pin and fit scalloped edging around edges of fabric so scallop will hang out over edges of canopy frame. Lift cut edge of scalloped edging and apply a thin line of fusible liquid adhesive ¼" from edges of fabric. Using iron, press to seal edges. Remove pins.

7. Place fabric on top of canopy frame, edging side up. Using a pencil, mark each corner for finials and, using razor blade, slit fabric at marks. Slide fabric over finials. Using hot-glue gun, adhere fabric to top of canopy frame, smoothing as you go.

8. Adhere satin rosebuds at regular intervals along top of canopy frame, covering "seam" of sealed fabric and edging.

Petite style: *crib dust ruffle*

YOU WILL NEED:
- Fabric scissors
- Hot-glue gun and glue sticks
- Lace: 2"-wide, threaded with ribbon for dust ruffle (12")
- Measuring tape
- Miniature crib with canopy
- Permanent liquid adhesive

MAKING THE PROJECT:

1. Using measuring tape, measure crib width of one end, along back, and width of remaining end, adding ½". Using fabric scissors, cut lace to those dimensions.

2. Place lace, wrong side up, on work surface. Apply a thin line of permanent liquid adhesive along short edges and fold each edge over ⅛" for finished edges.

3. Using hot-glue gun, dot-glue wrong side of straight edge of lace along one end of bed frame below mattress, across back, and along remaining end of crib.

Nighttime & naptime: *crib mattress*

YOU WILL NEED:
- Fabric: cotton print (5" x 7")
- Fabric scissors
- Miniature crib mattress
- Miniature crib with canopy
- Permanent liquid adhesive
- Straight-edge razor blade

MAKING THE PROJECT:

1. Remove mattress from crib. Using straight-edge razor blade, remove any existing fabrics from mattress.

2. Place fabric, wrong side up, on work surface. Center and place mattress on fabric. Using fabric scissors, cut fabric 2" larger than mattress all around.

3. Apply a thin line of permanent liquid adhesive along edges of mattress. Wrap edges of fabric up and adhere onto mattress. Allow to dry. Using fabric scissors, trim excess fabric from underside of mattress.

4. Place mattress, right side up, into crib.

Cozy comforter: *crib quilt*

YOU WILL NEED:
- Batting: flat
- Fabric: cotton print (6" x 12")
- Fabric scissors
- Fusible liquid adhesive
- Iron and ironing board
- Lace: ¼"-wide with decorative edge (12–14")
- Measuring tape
- Pressing cloth

MAKING THE PROJECT:

1. Using measuring tape, measure mattress width and length, adding ¼" to both measurements. Using fabric scissors, cut two fabric pieces to those dimensions.

2. Subtract ½" from each measurement and cut batting to those dimensions. Set aside.

3. Place one fabric piece, right side up, on work surface. Apply a thin line of fusible liquid adhesive ⅛" from edges. Place straight edge of lace, with decorative edge inward, onto adhesive. Do not pull lace tight at corners, allowing for curving when "quilt" is turned. Using iron and pressing cloth, press to seal, creating quilt top.

4. Place quilt top, wrong side up, on work surface. Fold edges over ¼" and press fold, leaving decorative edge of lace pointing away from fabric.

5. Place second fabric piece, wrong side up, on work surface. Apply a thin line of fusible liquid adhesive ⅛" from edges. Fold each edge over ¼". Press to seal edges.

6. Center and place batting onto wrong side of fabric. Carefully apply a thin line of fusible liquid adhesive along edges of fabric. Center and place quilt top, right side up, onto batting and fabric. Press to seal fabric pieces together and complete quilt.

Soothing slumber: *crib blanket*

YOU WILL NEED:
- Fabric: flannel (4" x 5")
- Fusible liquid adhesive
- Iron and ironing board
- Miniature crib
- Ribbon: ¼"-wide, satin (4")
- Pressing cloth

MAKING THE PROJECT:

1. Place fabric, right side up, on work surface. Apply a thin line of fusible liquid adhesive to wrong side of ribbon. Lay ribbon onto one short side of fabric, ½" from edge. Using iron and pressing cloth, press to seal.

2. Place fabric, wrong side up, on work surface. Apply a thin line of fusible liquid adhesive ¼" from long edges. Fold long sides of fabric to center of blanket and press to seal.

3. Hang blanket, right side up, with ribbon showing, over one end of crib.

Fleecy support: *crib pillow*

MAKING THE PROJECT:

1. Place fabric, wrong side up, on work surface. Apply a thin line of fusible liquid adhesive ⅛" from edges. Fold edges over ¼" and, using iron and pressing cloth, press to seal.

2. Using fabric scissors, cut batting ¼" smaller all around than fabric. Center and place batting onto fabric. Beginning at one short side, roll fabric and batting together into a ½"–1"-dia. "pillow roll."

3. Tie ribbon around center of pillow roll. Using fabric scissors, trim ribbon ends.

YOU WILL NEED:
- Batting: flat
- Fabric: eyelet (2" x 5")
- Fabric scissors
- Fusible liquid adhesive
- Iron and ironing board
- Pressing cloth
- Ribbon: ⅛"-wide (6")

Fresh start: *changing table cushion*

YOU WILL NEED:
- Batting: flat
- Fabric: cotton print (6" square)
- Fabric scissors
- Fusible liquid adhesive
- Iron and ironing board
- Measuring tape
- Miniature changing table
- Pressing cloth

MAKING THE PROJECT:

1. Using measuring tape, measure changing table top interior width and length, adding ¼" to each measurement. Using fabric scissors, cut two fabric pieces to those dimensions.

2. Subtract ⅛" from each measurement and cut batting to those dimensions.

3. Place one fabric piece, right side up, on work surface. Apply a thin line of fusible liquid adhesive ⅛" from one short edge and both long edges of fabric. Place second fabric piece, wrong side up, onto first fabric piece. Using an iron and pressing cloth, press to seal edges.

4. Turn sealed fabric pieces right side out. Insert batting into fabric. Turn remaining raw edges in ⅛". Apply a thin line fusible liquid adhesive along one inside edge and press to seal opening closed.

Play station: *toy chest*

YOU WILL NEED:
- Decorative miniatures: dolls, toys, etc.
- Fabric: cotton print
- Fabric scissors
- Fabric stiffening medium
- Hot-glue gun and glue sticks
- Measuring tape
- Miniature wooden chest: rectangular with an opening top

MAKING THE PROJECT:

1. Using measuring tape, measure around chest to determine length. Measure from chest bottom to highest point of chest to determine height. Using fabric scissors, cut fabric to those dimensions.

2. Saturate fabric with fabric stiffening medium. Lining up one long side of wet fabric at chest bottom, adhere one short side of fabric at center back of chest, wrap forward around front, and to center back of chest, slightly overlapping fabric ends. Using fabric scissors, trim around top edge of chest. Using your fingers, smooth out fabric while still wet. Allow to dry.

3. Add decorative miniatures in and around chest. Using hot-glue gun, adhere decorative miniatures to chest as desired.

Painted roses: *needlepoint floorcloth*

YOU WILL NEED:

- Acrylic paints: pink; red; green
- Fabric: Aida cloth (5" square)
- Fabric scissors
- Lace trim: ¼"-wide (½ yd.)
- Paintbrush: small, round
- Paper towels
- Permanent liquid adhesive

MAKING THE PROJECT:

1. Using fabric scissors, cut a 3½" x 4½" oval from Aida cloth.

2. Place oval, wrong side up, on work surface. Apply a thin line of permanent liquid adhesive ⅛" from edge. Place straight edge of lace trim, wrong side up, onto adhesive, slightly overlapping ends. Adhere ends together. Allow to dry.

3. Assume that the oval is a clock. Prepare to paint four roses on right side of oval at the 12 o'clock, 6 o'clock, 3 o'clock, and 9 o'clock positions.

4. Using paintbrush, apply an irregular circle of pink paint for each rose. Rinse paint-brush and blot water off with paper towel.

5. Apply red paint to center of pink circle. Rinse paintbrush and blot water off on paper towel.

6. Apply green paint to each side of pink circle, creating leaves. Apply paint for additional leaves as desired. Rinse paintbrush and blot water off with paper towel.

7. Repeat Steps 4–6 to complete center motif with one large rose and two smaller roses. Apply green paint in thin strokes to create crossed stems. Apply paint for additional leaves along each stem and at the base.

Visual interest:
nursery wall border

YOU WILL NEED:
- All-purpose adhesive
- Fabric scissors
- Measuring tape
- Ribbon: ¾"-wide, satin

MAKING THE PROJECT:

1. Using measuring tape, measure along top of back and side walls. Using fabric scissors, cut ribbon to those dimensions, adding 2"–3".

2. Apply all-purpose adhesive along one wall near ceiling. Fold ribbon end under ½" and adhere ribbon onto wall. Continue around room for remaining walls.

Comfort cushioning: *rocking chair cushion*

YOU WILL NEED:
- Batting: fluffy
- Button: ¼" dia., pearl with two holes (1)
- Fabric: cotton print (4" square)
- Fabric scissors
- Hot-glue gun and glue sticks
- Miniature rocking chair
- Sewing needle and coordinating thread

MAKING THE PROJECT:

1. Make the cushion following instructions for Buttoned Up: Decorator Pillow on Lounge on page 70 and using cotton print in place of crepe and lace.

2. Using hot-glue gun, adhere back of completed pillow to seat of rocking chair.

Swiss lace: *window treatment*

YOU WILL NEED:
- Acrylic paint: to match window
- Dowel: ⅛"-dia., 1" longer than width of window
- Eyescrews: gold (2)
- Fusible liquid adhesive
- Hammer
- Hot-glue gun and glue sticks
- Iron and ironing board
- Lace: 3"-wide, with scalloped edge (12"); ½"-wide, eyelet with ⅛" holes for threading (12")
- Nail: tiny
- Paintbrush: ¼" flat
- Pencil
- Pressing cloth
- Scissors: small
- Sculpting clay: coordinating color for dowel ball ends

MAKING THE PROJECT:

1. Place 3"-wide lace, wrong side up, on work surface. Apply a thin line of fusible liquid adhesive along one long edge of lace, ⅛" from edge. Place one right side edge of ½"-wide lace onto adhesive. Using an iron and pressing cloth, press to seal the two pieces of lace together.

2. Place sealed lace, wrong side up, on work surface. Apply a thin line of fusible liquid adhesive along short edges of combined lace and fold each end under ⅛". Press to seal edges.

3. Using paintbrush, paint dowel. Allow to dry.

4. Thread dowel through holes in adhered ½"-wide lace. If necessary, using small scissors, cut holes for easier threading.

5. Hold dowel up to window and, using pencil, mark placement for eyescrews. Allow at least ⅛" from each end of dowel to accommodate the ball ends.

6. Using hammer and tiny nail, make a small hole at each mark. Screw eyescrews into holes. Insert dowel, one end at a time, into eyescrews.

7. Roll a small bit of clay into two pea-sized balls. Poke each ball midway with one end of dowel. Remove dowel. Bake clay balls, following manufacturer's instructions. Allow to cool.

8. Using hot-glue gun, adhere one decorative ball to each end of dowel.

Cirque de enfant: *redecorating ideas*

Instead of using the traditional pastels and prints, give the nursery a more contemporary look by decorating with cheerful primary colors and bold geometric shapes.

Above: *Sew stenciled or purchased patterned ribbon to top edge of curtains and tie back with strings of brightly colored seed beads.*

Right: *Paint or stencil circus characters onto furniture pieces to coordinate with polk-a-dot ribbon in primary colors.*

Whimsy Bedroom

Entering the room of a teenage girl, is like stepping into another world. Bright colors, bold patterns, and eclectic collections reflect and fuel her drive for living life to its fullest.

Big pillows, teen magazines, and loyal pets are regulars in this house of style. Friends drop by for the latest girl-talk, loud music, and lots of giggling.

At the end of the school day, there is no better place than the comfy bed with its bright-colored blankets and huge geometric pillows to drop a book bag (and a tired body) and talk on the phone to her best friend, whom she hasn't seen for at least 10 minutes!

Her moods and her tastes are constantly changing. She puts posters up and takes them down again. It is here where she ponders over the important discoveries she makes about herself and the world around her in the process of becoming the woman of her dreams.

Whimsy Bedroom

The courageous blending of large prints, checks, and plaids results in a great hang out for the teen with a busy social life.

The vibrant colors and patterns found in the fabrics are borrowed to enliven the furniture. The chest of drawers, although identical in structure to the one in the nursery, takes on a personality of its own with the application of a bit of paint.

The pieced floorcloth and oversized ottoman placed at the foot of the bed on the pickled hardwood floor lends a timeless look to this energy charged atmosphere.

Above: *There is no such thing as ordinary here. For example, the oversized ottoman and woven chair command attention when visitors enter the room.*

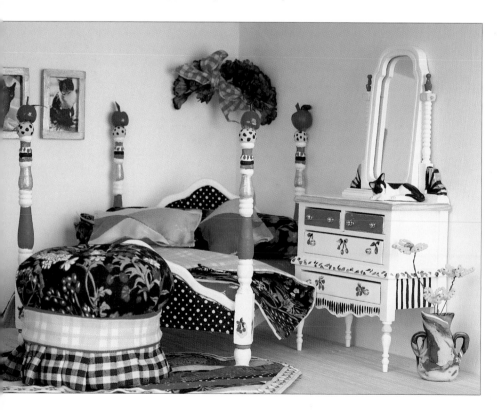

Left: *A comfortable four-poster bed is the focal point of this youthful bedroom—the perfect place to lounge with a favorite magazine in one hand and a telephone in the other.*

Clean & crisp: *whimsy sheet*

YOU WILL NEED:
- Fabric: cotton print
- Fabric scissors
- Fusible liquid adhesive
- Hot-glue gun and glue sticks
- Iron and ironing board
- Measuring tape
- Miniature four-poster bed
- Pins
- Pressing cloth
- Straight-edge razor blade

MAKING THE PROJECT:

1. Using a straight-edge razor blade, remove any existing fabrics from mattress.

2. Using measuring tape, measure from bottom of bed frame on one side to top of mattress, across mattress, and down other

side to bottom of bed frame. Measure from headboard to footboard, adding ½". Using fabric scissors, cut fabric to those dimensions.

3. Place fabric, wrong side up, on work surface. Apply a thin line of fusible liquid adhesive ⅛" from both long edges. Fold each edge over ¼" and, using iron and pressing cloth, press to seal edges.

4. Fold fabric in half lengthwise with sealed edges together. Pin at each end to mark center. Unfold fabric. Using measuring tape, measure width of mattress near headboard and footboard and pin at each end to mark center. Place center of fabric top and bottom on center of mattress top and bottom. Remove all pins. Wrap fabric firmly from center around to one side of bed. Using hot-glue gun, adhere wrapped edge along bottom of bed frame.

5. Smooth fabric across mattress and wrap remaining edge over other side of bed. Adhere wrapped edge along bottom of bed frame.

6. Using thin smooth object, tuck top and bottom of fabric in between mattress and headboard and footboard to hide raw edges.

Change of mood: *reversible coverlet*

You will need:
- Batting: fluffy
- Fabric: cotton prints, ⅓ yd. (2)
- Fabric scissors
- Fusible liquid adhesive
- Iron and ironing board
- Measuring tape
- Miniature four-poster bed
- Pressing cloth

Making the project:
1. Using measuring tape, measure from bottom of bed frame on one side to top of mattress, across mattress, and down other side to bottom of bed frame, adding ½". Measure from headboard to footboard, adding ½". Using fabric scissors, cut both print fabrics to those dimensions.

2. Cut batting ⅛" smaller all around than fabrics.

3. Place one fabric piece, right side up, on work surface. Apply a thin line of fusible liquid adhesive ⅛" from one short edge and both long edges of fabric. Place second fabric piece, wrong side up, onto first fabric piece. Using iron and pressing cloth, press to seal edges together.

4. Turn sealed fabric pieces right side out. Insert batting into fabric. Turn remaining raw edges inward. Apply a thin line fusible liquid adhesive along one inside edge and press to seal opening closed.

Bright bolster: *large pillow roll*

YOU WILL NEED:
- Batting: fluffy
- Fabric: cotton print
- Fabric scissors
- Fusible liquid adhesive
- Iron and ironing board
- Measuring tape
- Pressing cloth
- Ribbon: ⅛"-wide, satin (12")

MAKING THE PROJECT:

1. Using measuring tape, measure width of headboard, adding 2". Using fabric scissors, cut fabric to those dimensions and 3" long.

2. Place fabric, wrong side up, on work surface. Apply a thin line of fusible liquid adhesive ⅛" from both short edges of fabric. Fold edges over ¼" and, using iron and pressing cloth, press to seal edges.

3. Place fabric, right side up, on work surface. Apply a thin line of fusible liquid adhesive ⅛" from one long edge of fabric. Fold fabric in half lengthwise, right sides together. Press to seal edges together, creating a tube. Allow to cool.

4. Turn tube right side out. Stuff tube with batting to 1" from each end. Using fabric scissors, cut ribbon into two equal pieces. Tie one ribbon piece in a knot ¾" from one end of roll. Continue stuffing tube to ¾" from remaining end. Tie remaining ribbon in a knot at remaining end. Trim all ribbon ends to about ½".

Silken accents: *toss pillows*

SEE PHOTO ON PAGE 107.

You will need:
- Batting: fluffy
- Fabric: silk scraps
- Fabric scissors
- Fusible liquid adhesive
- Iron and ironing board
- Pressing cloth

MAKING THE PROJECT:

1. Using fabric scissors, cut fabric scraps into geometrical shapes. Place one shape, right side up, on work surface. Apply a thin line of fusible liquid adhesive ⅛" from one edge of shape. Place one edge of second shape, wrong side up, onto adhesive. Using iron and pressing cloth, press to seal edges. Continue in this manner until fabric is pieced as desired. Using fabric scissors, cut pieced fabric into 3" squares.

2. Place one pieced square, right side up, on work surface. Apply a thin line of fusible liquid adhesive ⅛" from three edges of square. Place another pieced square, wrong side up, onto adhesive. Using iron, press to seal fabric squares together. Allow to cool.

3. Turn sealed fabric squares right side out. Stuff with batting.

4. Turn remaining raw edges inward. Apply a thin line of fusible liquid adhesive along one inside edge and, press to seal opening closed.

Stripes, dots & checks: *fabric floorcloth*

YOU WILL NEED:
- Fabric: cotton prints (5)
- Fabric marking pen
- Fusible liquid adhesive
- Iron and ironing board
- Paper: white
- Pencil
- Pressing cloth
- Ribbon: fanciful design
- Rotary cutter
- Scissors: craft; fabric

MAKING THE PROJECT:

1. Using rotary cutter, cut four ¾" strips, 8" long from each fabric on the straight of the weave.

2. Place one strip, right side up, on work surface.

3. Apply a thin line of fusible liquid adhesive ⅛" from one long edge. Place a strip of a different print, wrong side up, on top of first strip. Using iron and pressing cloth, press for 30 seconds to seal. Allow to cool.

4. Open strips and place, right side up, on work surface. Place pressing cloth over both strips and, using iron, press flat.

5. Apply a thin line of fusible liquid adhesive ⅛" from remaining long edge of second strip. Place a strip of a different print, wrong side up, on top of second strip. Press for 30 seconds to seal. Allow to cool. Continue in this manner until all strips are pieced and sealed together.

6. Using pencil, draw a 5" x 6" rectangle on paper. Using craft scissors, cut out. Cut off each corner 1" from point for an octagon-shaped pattern.

7. Place pieced fabric, right side up, on work surface. Place paper pattern diagonally on pieced fabric. Using fabric marking pen, trace around pattern. Using fabric scissors, cut out.

8. Place one print fabric, right side up, on work surface. Place pattern on fabric. Using fabric pen, trace around pattern, adding ¼" all around. Using fabric scissors, cut out.

9. Place print fabric octagon, wrong side up, on work surface. Apply a thin line of fusible liquid adhesive ⅛" from edges. Fold edges over ¼" and, using iron and pressing cloth, press to seal edges.

10. Place pieced fabric octagon, wrong side up, on work surface. Apply a thin line of fusible liquid adhesive ¼" from edges. Place print fabric octagon, right side up, onto adhesive. Press to seal fabrics together.

11. Finish by applying a dot of fusible liquid adhesive ¼" from one edge of pieced fabric. Place one end of ribbon onto adhesive. Press to adhere ribbon. Continue around all edges of pieced fabric, dot-gluing and ironing as you go. Square off corners and slightly overlap ribbon ends.

Satin basketweave: *seat covering*

YOU WILL NEED:
- Corrugated cardboard: (6" square)
- Fabric scissors
- Miniature chair
- Pins
- Permanent liquid adhesive
- Ribbon: ⅛"-wide, satin, two colors (1 yd. each)

MAKING THE PROJECT:

1. Using fabric scissors, cut 24 pieces of ribbon, 3" long.

2. Alternating colors, pin one end of 12 ribbons close together, from left to right, along top side of cardboard. Pin one end of remaining ribbons close together, from top to bottom, along left side of cardboard.

3. Beginning with the top ribbon on the left side, weave over and under ribbons pinned along the top side. Alternately weave all ribbons to create the chair seat cover.

4. Apply a thin line of permanent liquid adhesive along ribbon ends to secure. Remove pins and trim ribbon ends to fit chair seat. Apply a dot of permanent liquid adhesive to wrong side of woven chair seat cover. Adhere to seat.

Oversize lounging: *large ottoman*

YOU WILL NEED:
- Batting: fluffy
- Buttons: ½"-wide with two holes (2)
- Drill and ⅛" drill bit
- Fabric: cotton prints (3)
- Fabric scissors
- Fusible liquid adhesive
- Hot-glue gun and glue sticks
- Iron and ironing board
- Needle with large eye
- Permanent liquid adhesive
- Pins
- Plastic lid to aerosol can
- Pressing cloth
- Ribbon: ¾"-wide, (10"); ⅛"-wide, satin (18")

MAKING THE PROJECT:

1. Using fabric scissors, cut a 5¼"-dia. circle from one print fabric. Cut a 2" x 15" piece from second print fabric. Cut a 1" x 9" strip from third print fabric.

2. Using drill and ⅛" drill bit, make a small hole through center of plastic lid.

3. Using hot-glue gun, adhere top of plastic lid to batting. Adhere batting around upper half of lid sides. Using fabric scissors, trim batting around lid.

4. Thread needle with ⅛"-wide ribbon. Pull ribbon to double. Take needle through one hole of one button, through center of fabric circle with right side up, down through batting and hole in lid, and then through one hole of the remaining button, pulling it snugly up into the lid.

5. Take needle up through second hole of second button, through hole in lid and batting, through center of fabric circle, and through second hole of first button. Cinch ribbon ends up tightly and tie in double knot. Using fabric scissors, cut ribbon ends close to knot.

6. Assume fabric circle is a clock. Pull fabric taut at 12 o'clock and, using hot-glue gun, adhere to bottom of lid side. Repeat for 6 o'clock, 3 o'clock, and 9 o'clock positions. Continue dot-gluing between these four points to evenly distribute the gathering of the fabric around the lid.

7. Fold long piece of fabric in half lengthwise. Using iron, press along fold. Pleat and pin the doubled fabric so ½" folds will show all around the ottoman. Press pleats. Apply a dot of permanent liquid adhesive at each pleat along raw edge of fabric. Wrap pleated fabric around lid and slightly overlap ends. Using fabric scissors, cut to necessary length. Remove pleated fabric from lid. Apply a thin line of fusible liquid adhesive to underside of overlapping short end. Fold end under and, using iron and pressing cloth, press to seal edge.

8. Reposition pleated fabric around lid so folded pleats sweep the floor. Using hot-glue gun, adhere fabric to lid.

9. Wrap ¾"-wide ribbon around ottoman and, using hot-glue gun, adhere ribbon over raw edges of pleated fabric.

10. Fold long edges of remaining fabric strip to center and, using iron, press folds. Center and adhere strip over ¾"-wide ribbon.

A pear of arches: *window treatment*

YOU WILL NEED:
- Acrylic paints: to match window
- Acrylic spray sealer
- Dowel: ⅛"-dia., 1" longer than width of window
- Eyescrews: gold, (2)
- Fabric: cotton print (8" x 13")
- Fusible liquid adhesive
- Fabric scissors
- Hammer
- Hot-glue gun and glue sticks
- Iron and ironing board
- Measuring tape
- Nail: tiny
- Paintbrush: flat
- Paper: white (1 sheet)
- Pencil
- Pins
- Pressing cloth
- Ribbon: ⅛"-wide, satin (13")
- Sculpting clay
- Silk leaf

MAKING THE PROJECT:

1. Enlarge Whimsy Window Pattern. Using pencil, trace onto white paper. Fold fabric in half lengthwise, wrong sides together. Place paper pattern on fold. Pin pattern in place. Using fabric scissors, cut out around pattern. Remove pattern and pins.

2. Apply a thin line of fusible liquid adhesive ½" from fold. Place ribbon onto adhesive. Using iron and pressing cloth, press to seal. Allow to cool.

3. Open fabric and place, wrong side up, on work surface. Apply a thin line of fusible liquid adhesive ⅛" from edges. Fold edges over ¼" and press to seal.

4. Fold fabric in half lengthwise again, wrong sides together, and press fold.

5. Open fabric. Using measuring tape, measure ¼" from fold. Apply a thin straight line of fusible liquid adhesive parallel to the fold. Fold fabric again, being careful to avoid dragging fabric through wet adhesive. Using iron and pressing cloth, press to seal. Allow to cool.

6. Open fabric again to check seal. Using measuring tape, measure ¼" from the seal and apply another thin line of fusible liquid

adhesive. Fold fabric again and, using iron and pressing cloth, press to seal, leaving a channel for dowel to thread through.

7. Apply a thin line of fusible liquid adhesive down one short edge to point, along curve to point, and up remaining short edge. Press to seal fabric together.

8. Using paintbrush, paint dowel. Allow to dry.

9. Thread dowel through fabric channel. Hold dowel up to window and, using pencil, mark placement for eyescrews. Allow at least $\frac{1}{4}$" from each end of dowel to accommodate pear ends.

10. Using hammer and tiny nail, make a small hole at each mark. Screw eyescrews into holes. Insert dowel, one end at a time, into eyescrews.

11. Roll a bit of clay into two lima bean-sized balls. Gently form into pear shape. Slightly flatten each pear bottom.

12. Poke each pear's side midway with one end of dowel. Remove dowel. Bake clay pears, following manufacturer's instructions. Allow to cool.

13. Paint clay pears as desired. Allow to dry. Spray with acrylic sealer. Allow to dry.

14. Using fabric scissors, cut two leaves to scale of clay pears from silk leaf. Using hot-glue gun, adhere one leaf to each pear top. Adhere a pear to each dowel end.

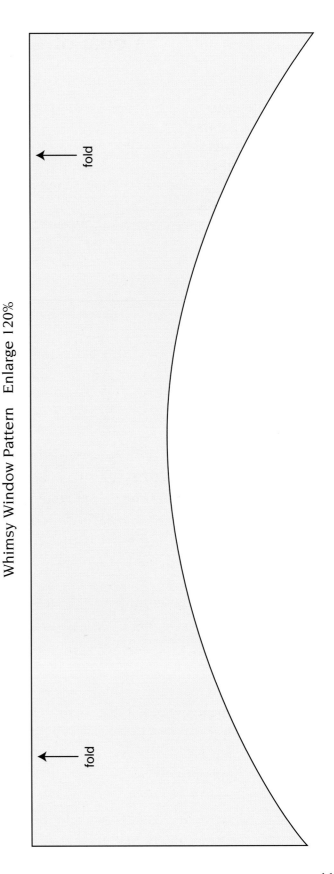

Whimsy Window Pattern   Enlarge 120%

fold

fold

Wild side: *redecorating ideas*

This themed room goes right to the heart of Africa. Natural colors and prints are accented with a touch of red that unifies the room and adds spice to the space.

Above: *Make animal heads from sculpting clay to decorate curtain rod ends.*

Left: *Cover the floor by adhering crumpled bits of brown paper with découpage medium. Make mask on wall and animal heads on bed posts and chest of drawers from sculpting clay. Use animal prints to make bedding and floorcloth.*

Patio
Furniture

tea party

family

terrace

flagstones

picnic

nature

siesta

outside

lemonade

In the good old summertime when all the world is green, the cobblestone path leads to the patio.

The chaise lounge is built for watching the puffy white clouds roll by. There's just enough time for an afternoon "snooze" before the neighbors arrive for the barbeque.

It's the perfect party place for celebrating the annual blooming of the roses. Their familiar fragrance mixes with the delicate, sweet scent of jasmine blossoms permeating the warm air. Humming birds flit from flower to flower, sipping the nectar of the clematis that has climbed its way up and around the arbor.

The family cocker spaniel sits close by, enjoying the company of family and friends. A pitcher full of lemonade and a favorite board game are set out on the covered table in preparation for making memories that will last a lifetime.

Patio
Furniture

The yellow ribbons and potted daisies pleasantly complement the blue and white plaid cushions and covers on the patio furniture.

The addition of the fish motif expresses a feeling for being outdoors—spending lazy days reading magazines and balmy nights watching shooting stars.

Above: *A fish motif was chosen to accent the blue plaid cushions on the patio furniture.*

Left: *The blue wood siding harmoniously combines with shutters and inset stones to give the exterior of the dollhouse a natural feel.*

Plaid party: *table cover*

You will need:
- Fabric: cotton print (5" square)
- Fabric scissors
- Fusible liquid adhesive
- Iron and ironing board
- Miniature round patio table
- Permanent liquid adhesive
- Pressing cloth
- Ribbon: ⅛"-wide (24")

Making the project:

1. Place fabric, wrong side up, on work surface. Apply a thin line of fusible liquid adhesive ⅛" from edges. Fold edges over ⅛" and, using iron and pressing cloth, press to seal edges.

2. Using fabric scissors, cut ribbon into four equal pieces. Place fabric square, wrong side up, on work surface.

3. Refer to Corner Diagram. Measure ½" from one corner toward center and apply a dot fusible liquid adhesive. Fold one ribbon in half to find its center and set that point onto adhesive so ribbon crosses corner. Using iron and pressing cloth, press to seal ribbon to fabric. Allow to cool. Repeat for each ribbon on each corner.

4. Turn fabric over, right side up, on work surface. Tie each ribbon into a tiny bow, gathering each corner of fabric. Secure each bow with a dot of permanent liquid adhesive. Trim excess ribbon. Place cover on miniature table.

Note: The tie at each corner keeps cover in place on patio table when the "wind" blows.

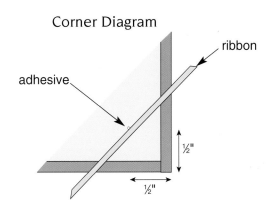

Corner Diagram

121

Outdoor comfort: *chair & chaise lounge cushions*

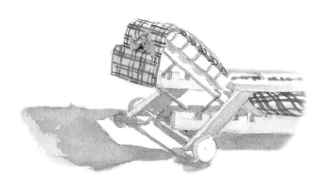

YOU WILL NEED:
- Batting: flat
- Fabric: cotton print; cotton with small print (2–3")
- Fabric scissors
- Fusible liquid adhesive
- Iron and ironing board
- Measuring tape
- Pins
- Pressing cloth

MAKING THE PROJECT:

1. Using measuring tape, measure width and length of chair or lounge seat and back, doubling length, then adding ¼" to width and length. Add another 1½" to length for back cushion if a magazine holder is desired. Using fabric scissors, cut fabric to those dimensions.

2. Place fabric, wrong side up, on work surface. Apply a thin line of fusible liquid adhesive ⅛" from edges. Fold edges over ¼" and, using iron and pressing cloth, seal edges.

3. Using fabric scissors, cut batting slightly smaller than half the length of fabric after edges are sealed for each cushion. Center and place batting on one half of fabric.

Apply a thin line of fusible liquid adhesive ⅛" from fabric edges. Fold remaining half of fabric over and, using iron and pressing cloth, press to seal.

. Using fabric scissors, cut out motif from print fabric.

. Place motif, wrong side up, on work surface. Apply a thin line of fusible liquid adhesive ⅛" from edges. Center and place motif, right side up, onto cushion and, using iron and pressing cloth, press to seal. Repeat for all cushions.

6. Refer to Cushion Back Diagram. To finish back cushion with magazine holder, place cushion on chair or lounge back with fabric for holder wrong side up and hanging over back. Fold fabric, wrong sides together, to create a pocket for magazine. Pin at fold to mark center and remove cushion from chair or lounge. Open fabric. Apply a thin line of fusible liquid adhesive ⅛" from side edges from short end of fabric to fold. Fold fabric again and, using iron and pressing cloth, press to seal fabric, forming pocket.

Cushion Back Diagram

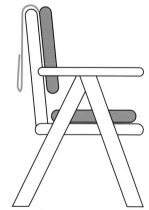

Garden party: *redecorating ideas*

Trade masculine plaids for feminine florals to decorate this garden picnic scene. The colors found in the fabric and ribbon coordinate with the flowers planted outside.

Above: *Make blinds by folding colored paper to make pleats, piercing pleats with needle and thread, and pulling threads up to top of paper to gather blind.*

Left: *Make a garden pond by gluing small stones around a small round mirror. Adhere a purchased miniature garden ornament to the center of the mirror.*

Hats off: *acknowledgments*

Several projects in this book were created with outstanding and innovative products developed by the following manufacturers: DecoArts Americana Paints of Stanford, Kentucky, for all acrylic paints; Signature Crafts Marketing of Hawthorn, New Jersey, for Beacon Adhesives (Liqui-Fuse™ and Fabri-Tac™ adhesives); Walmar Dollhouses of Alexandria, Virginia, for the unique shell of a dollhouse; and Woodland Sales of Scottsdale, Arizona, for Quick Grab® Inc. adhesive. We would like to offer our sincere appreciation to these companies for the valuable support given in this ever changing industry of new ideas, concepts, designs, and products.

A very warm thank you to our brother and his wife, Spencer and Peggy Combe, and their family for allowing us to photograph the dollhouse in its entirety in their lovely home. Thank you Chelsey Ann for letting us photograph your beautiful bedroom!

Relative values: *metric conversion chart*

mm-millimetres cm-centimetres
inches to millimetres and centimetres

inches	mm	cm	inches	cm	inches	cm
⅛	3	0.3	9	22.9	30	76.2
¼	6	0.6	10	25.4	31	78.7
½	13	1.3	12	30.5	33	83.8
⅝	16	1.6	13	33.0	34	86.4
¾	19	1.9	14	35.6	35	88.9
⅞	22	2.2	15	38.1	36	91.4
1	25	2.5	16	40.6	37	94.0
1¼	32	3.2	17	43.2	38	96.5
1½	38	3.8	18	45.7	39	99.1
1¾	44	4.4	19	48.3	40	101.6
2	51	5.1	20	50.8	41	104.1
2½	64	6.4	21	53.3	42	106.7
3	76	7.6	22	55.9	43	109.2
3½	89	8.9	23	58.4	44	111.8
4	102	10.2	24	61.0	45	114.3
4½	114	11.4	25	63.5	46	116.8
5	127	12.7	26	66.0	47	119.4
6	152	15.2	27	68.6	48	121.9
7	178	17.8	28	71.1	49	124.5
8	203	20.3	29	73.7	50	127.0

In other words: *index*

A pear of arches: window treatment 114
Austrian poof: window treatment 39
Bath beads & baubles: bath accessories 50
Beauty in damask: bedspread 66
Bright bolster: large pillow roll 107
Buttoned up: decorator pillow on lounge 70
Casual chic: redecorating ideas 40
Cirque de enfant: redecorating ideas 100
Change of mood: reversible coverlet 106
Check out: redecorating ideas 54
Cheques & fleurs: refrigerator runner 24
Clean & crisp: whimsy sheet 105
Couturère: pedestal & draped mannequin 84
Comfort cushioning: rocking chair cushion 98
Cozy comforter: crib quilt 93
Creative retreat: window treatment 85
Creativity prevails: redecorating ideas 86
Crumb catchers: napkins 23
Daily accent: table runner 23
Elegant adornment: lace canopy 59
Eye-pleasing partitions: fabric-covered walls 72
Fabric Tips 11
Fancy reflection: oval mirror 68
Fleecy support: crib pillow 94
Formal stripes: table runner 35
Frame embellishment: bedpost tassels 67
Fresh start: changing table cushion 95
Fringed edges: area rug 35
Garden Bathroom 44–55
Garden lattice: wall design 51
Garden party: redecorating ideas 124
General Information 8–15
General Materials Needed 13
Helpful Hints 14
Introduction 8
Lace trimmings: pâtisserie cupboard 20
Le coq: redecorating ideas 26
Linen roses: decorator pillows 34
Living & Dining Room 28–43
Luxurious wrap: afghan 71
Making a Circle Using a Compass 15

Master Suite 56–75
Mild manners: puddled table covering 31
Natty notions: fabric & trims in cupboard 79
New-found flowers: covered chest of drawers 47
Nighttime & naptime: crib mattress 92
Outdoor comfort: chair & chaise lounge cushions 122
Oversize lounging: large ottoman 113
Painted roses: needlepoint floorcloth 97
Patio Furniture 118–125
Petite cheques: chair cushion 24
Petite style: crib dust ruffle 92
Plaid party: table cover 121
Play station: toy chest 96
Possible Places to Find Tiny Items 13
Pretty percale: top sheet 62
Pretty-n-pink Nursery 88–101
Proper headrest: bed pillows 64
Provence Kitchen 16–27
Quiet mood: lamp shade 71
Quilt of generations: redecorating ideas 74
Rags to riches: circular braided rag rug 48
Ribboned cluster: hat boxes 83
Rolled up: window treatment 53
Satin basketweave: seat covering 112
Satin rosebuds: crib canopy 91
Scraps & snips: cutting table 82
Sewing Room 76–87
Silken accents: toss pillows 108
Simply sheer: window treatment 25
Sitting pretty: small stool 83
Soothing slumber: crib blanket 94
Soft & fluffy: bath mat 50
Soft touch: bath towels 48
Storage solution: suede trunk 81
Stripes, dots & checks: fabric floorcloth 108
Swiss lace: window treatment 99
Tea rose: kitchen china 21
Textile treasures: fabric rolls 80
Things That are Useful 13
Tiny stitches: embroidery hoop 70
Touch of brass: window treatment 73
Tucked away: bottom sheet 61
Victorian detail: shirred headboard 60
Visual interest: nursery wall border 98
Wainscotting: wall decor & chair railing 36
Whimsy Bedroom 102–117
White on white: custom sofa & chairs 32
Wild side: redecorating ideas 116
Woven fibers: hutch blanket 36